JOURNEYS

Write-In Reader

Grade 3

Printed in the U.S.A.

ISBN 978-0-547-87421-0

40 41 0607 24 23

4500868730   A B C D E F G

Be a Reading Detective!

Welcome to your *Write-In Reader*! With this book, you will be a **Reading Detective**. You will look for clues in stories and in nonfiction selections. The clues will help you

- ▶ **enjoy stories,**

- ▶ **understand nonfiction,**

- ▶ **answer questions, and**

- ▶ **be a great reader!**

A Reading Detective can solve the mystery of any reading selection. No selection is too hard! A Reading Detective **asks questions**. A Reading Detective **reads carefully**.

Asking questions and reading carefully will help you **find clues**. Then, you will

- ▶ **stop,**

- ▶ **think, and**

- ▶ **write!**

Let's try it! Follow the trail . . .

Try It !

In the box is the beginning of a story. Read carefully. Ask yourself questions:

▶ **Who is the story about?**

▶ **Where and when does the story take place?**

▶ **What is happening?**

Look for clues to answer your questions.

> Logan was enjoying his bike ride. He felt the warm sun on his face. He smelled the beach nearby. He heard his dad humming on the bike in front of him. So far, Logan was having a great birthday.
>
> Suddenly, Logan screeched to a stop.
>
> "Dad!" he called out. "Look at that!"

Stop Think Write

Where and when does the story take place? How do you know?

_____

_____

Did you read carefully? Did you look for clues? Did the clues help you answer the questions? If they did, you are already a **Reading Detective**!

Contents

Unit 1

Lesson 1 2
Icos Goes to School 4

Lesson 2 12
The Trial of John Peter Zenger 14

Lesson 3 22
Not Just a Little! 24

Lesson 4 32
Building a New Barn 34

Lesson 5 42
Let's Play Ball! 44

Unit 2

Lesson 6 52
Owls 54

Lesson 7 62
Douglas Florian's Books 64

Lesson 8 72
Living Things Are Linked 74

Lesson 9 82
Puppets Around the World 84

Lesson 10 92
Aleck's Big Ideas 94

Unit 3

Lesson 11 102
Sports, Exactly 104

Lesson 12 112
Anansi's Bad Hair Day 114

Lesson 13 122
Little Mud-Face 124

Lesson 14 132
Dogs That Help 134

Lesson 15 142
Swedish Meatball Potstickers
  with Mustard Dipping Sauce 144

Unit 4

Lesson 16 152
Mark's Idea. 154

Lesson 17 162
Mammoths Long Ago and Today 164

Lesson 18 172
The Life of a Hickory Tree 174

Lesson 19 182
The Enchanted Flute 184

Lesson 20 192
A World of Ice 194

Unit 5

Lesson 21 202
The Jimjick King. 204

Lesson 22 212
Snow Petrels. 214

Lesson 23 222
Dog of the Future 224

Lesson 24 232
To the South Seas 234

Lesson 25 242
Ski Patrol 244

Unit 6

Lesson 26 252
The Race of 1903 254

Lesson 27 262
The Boy Who Made the TV 264

Lesson 28 272
Climbing the Slopes. 274

Lesson 29 282
Sprinting Joyce. 284

Lesson 30 292
The Rockets 294

✓ **TARGET VOCABULARY**

certainly
fine
proud
strolled

Athens, Greece

Check the answer.

1 Long ago, Athens, Greece, had many beautiful buildings. The people of Athens were _____ of their city.

☐ **sore** ☐ **proud** ☐ **empty**

2 People often met outdoors. They _____ through the streets. They stood in the marketplace. They talked about ideas and art.

☐ **strolled** ☐ **overlooked** ☐ **accepted**

3 Even today, Athens is _____ a place worth visiting. Visitors are sure to enjoy the statues and buildings from long ago.

☐ **lonely** ☐ **special** ☐ **certainly**

2

4 Describe how a <u>fine</u> day would look to you.

_____

_____

_____

5 Tell about a place where you <u>strolled</u> recently.

_____

_____

_____

Icos Goes to School

by Margaret Maugenest

Morning, 400 B.C.E.
Athens, Greece

Doran shook the sleeping boy. "Time to get up, Icos," he said. "It's going to be fine, sunny weather."

Icos yawned and turned over. "It's always fine weather in Athens," he said. "So what?"

"You must get up," Doran said firmly. "It's time for school."

Stop   Think   Write

STORY STRUCTURE

When and where does the story take place?

_____

_____

_____

Icos sighed. It was barely light out. He didn't want to get up. It took him a while to get out of bed.

Doran walked to school with Icos. Doran was Icos's servant. The two strolled through the streets.

They reached the school late. The teacher was already sitting on his tall chair. Icos sat on a bench at the back. Doran stayed outside.

Stop Think Write

CAUSE AND EFFECT

Why doesn't Icos rush to get ready?

_____

_____

_____

The teacher gave each student a block of wax. It was time to practice writing. Icos looked for his stylus.

Doran came in with the stylus. Now Icos could carve letters into the wax. Icos tried not to yawn. He was **proud** of his tidy writing. He wanted to do a good job.

Stop   Think   Write

Why is Icos proud of his writing?

_____

_____

_____

By now, Icos was wide awake. It was time to learn a poem. This poem was not written down. The teacher spoke each line. The students repeated it.

The teacher called on Icos to say the whole poem. Icos stood. He spoke in a firm voice. He did not leave one word out.

Doran came in. He took the writing stylus back. "You certainly did well!" he told Icos.

Stop Think Write

VOCABULARY

What other word could Doran use that has the same meaning as <u>certainly</u>?

_____

_____

_____

7

Now it was music time. One student played the harp. Another played the flute. Icos and the other boys sang.

Icos looked out at the servants. Doran was nodding in time to the music. The teacher was tapping his foot. "We must be doing well," Icos thought.

Stop Think Write

CAUSE AND EFFECT

What makes Icos think that the students are playing the music well?

_____

_____

_____

The afternoon was for sports. The boys walked to the sports field. Their servants came with them. The field was at the edge of the city.

The boys worked hard. Building strong bodies was important. They ran races. They jumped. Sports teachers watched them. Icos won a race. He was very pleased.

Stop | Think | Write

STORY STRUCTURE

Where do the boys practice sports?

_____

_____

_____

At last the school day ended. Icos and Doran walked home together. "That was a full day," Icos said.

"Yes, it was," Doran agreed. "You had fun at school, didn't you?" he asked.

Icos knew what Doran was saying. "Yes, I did. I'll try not to be so slow and grumpy tomorrow morning!"

Stop Think Write

UNDERSTANDING CHARACTERS

How does Icos feel about his day?

Look Back and Respond

1 Name one way that Doran is helpful to Icos.

Hint

For clues, see pages 4, 6, and 7.

_____

_____

_____

2 How does Icos change at the end of the story?

Hint

For clues, see page 10.

_____

_____

_____

3 What clues in the pictures show that the story takes place long ago?

Hint

Clues are on every page.

_____

_____

_____

Be a Reading Detective!

"A Fine, Fine School"
Student Book pp. 15–33

1 Who creates a problem in this story?

☐ the teachers ☐ Tillie

☐ Mr. Keene

Prove It! What evidence in the story supports your answer? Check the boxes. ☑ Make notes.

Evidence	Notes
☐ what makes the characters unhappy	
☐ what the teachers do and say	
☐ what Tillie does and says	
☐ what Mr. Keene does and says	

Write About It!

STORY STRUCTURE

Answer question **1** using evidence from the text.

_____

_____

_____

_____

_____

_____

_____

2 **When did Tillie go to Mr. Keene?**

☐ right after the first Saturday of school

☐ right after the first Sunday of school

☐ on the first day of summer

Prove It! What evidence in the story supports your answer? Check the boxes. ☑ Make notes.

Evidence	Notes
☐ text about the event	
☐ signal words	
☐ the illustrations	

Write About It!

SEQUENCE OF EVENTS

Answer question 2 using evidence from the text.

_____

_____

_____

_____

_____

_____

_____

✔ **TARGET VOCABULARY**

guilty
honest
jury
trial

What Happens in a Court?

1 What if a person is accused of a crime? She might say, "I am not guilty." In a court, people try to find out if she is telling the truth.

What other word could someone use to say that she is not guilty?

_____

_____

2 A trial gives both sides a chance to tell what they believe happened. Lawyers ask questions to try to learn the truth.

Why is it important to hear both sides in a trial?

_____

_____

_____

3 Most people try very hard to be **honest** in court. They tell the truth when a question is asked.

Write a word that means the opposite of <u>honest</u>.

_____

4 Twelve people are on the **jury**. They decide if the person did the crime or not. Everyone on the jury must agree.

Why do you think a <u>jury</u> has twelve people instead of just one person?

_____

_____

_____

The Trial of John Peter Zenger

by Lois Grippo

A Stamp for Eastchester

School children in the town of Eastchester, New York, want a special postage stamp. They want a stamp of a man named John Peter Zenger. John Zenger was once put on trial in Eastchester. He was put on trial because he told the truth!

| Stop | Think | Write |

VOCABULARY

Why was the <u>trial</u> of John Peter Zenger unusual?

_____

_____

_____

An Unfair Leader

The trial of John Peter Zenger took place in 1735. America was still part of England. The governor of New York was a man named William Cosby. People in New York did not pick Cosby. He was sent from England.

William Cosby would not let some men vote. This made people in Eastchester very angry. They wanted others to know that Cosby was unfair.

Stop **Think** **Write**

INFER AND PREDICT

Why might people want a governor they choose themselves?

_____

_____

_____

John Peter Zenger Speaks Out

John Peter Zenger ran a newspaper. He wrote in his paper about William Cosby. Everyone who read the paper learned of Governor Cosby's unfair actions.

Governor Cosby had Zenger put in jail! He said that the stories in Zenger's newspaper told lies. He claimed that the lies hurt him. Zenger stayed in jail for ten months before he even had a trial.

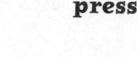

a printing press

Stop   Think   Write

CONCLUSIONS

Do you think that William Cosby was a good governor? Explain.

_____

_____

_____

Trial by Jury

At last the trial began. A jury would decide if John Zenger was guilty. Did he tell lies that hurt Governor Cosby? If he did, the jury would have to say he was guilty.

The jury heard the governor's side of the story first. They heard about Zenger's newspaper stories. They were told that no one had the right to print bad things about the governor.

Stop   Think   Write

VOCABULARY

What was the job of the jury in John Zenger's trial?

_____

_____

_____

Zenger's Story

A lawyer told John Zenger's side of the story. "What you heard was true," he said. "The stories in the paper did say bad things about the governor."

The lawyer didn't stop there. "However, the stories were honest," he said. "They told the truth about what Governor Cosby did."

Stop Think Write

If the stories were <u>honest</u>, did John Zenger tell lies?

_____

_____

_____

A Big Decision

Finally, both sides were finished. The people on the jury thought about all they had heard. Then they made their decision.

It only took the jury ten minutes to make up their minds. They said that John Peter Zenger was not guilty!

Stop **Think** **Write**

SUMMARIZE

What was the big decision?

_____

_____

_____

Remembering a Leader

John Peter Zenger was a leader. The men in the jury were leaders, too. They stood up for the right to tell the truth.

That is why the children of Eastchester want a postage stamp. They want to remind us of the trial of John Peter Zenger. They want to remind us of a right that keeps our country strong.

Stop · Think · Write

CONCLUSIONS

Do you think that a stamp of John Peter Zenger is a good idea? Explain.

_____

_____

_____

Look Back and Respond

1 How was John Peter Zenger a leader? Explain.

Hint
For clues, see pages 16 and 20.

_____

_____

_____

2 Why do you think the jury took only ten minutes to decide that John Peter Zenger was not guilty?

Hint
For clues, see page 18.

_____

_____

_____

3 How do the children of Eastchester show that they care about people from their town's past?

Hint
For clues, see page 14.

_____

_____

_____

Be a Reading Detective!

1 **Who tries the hardest to find out the truth about the pie?**

☐ Mrs. Brown   ☐ the judge   ☐ the jury

☐ other _____

Prove It! What evidence in the story supports your answer? Check the boxes. ☑ Make notes.

Evidence	Notes
☐ what Mrs. Brown says and does	
☐ what the judge says and does	
☐ what jury members say and do	
☐ the illustrations	

Write About It!

CONCLUSIONS

Answer question ❶ using evidence from the text.

_____

_____

_____

_____

_____

_____

2 **What caused the pie to fall into the bushes?**

☐ The judge put it there.

☐ Mrs. Brown dropped it by mistake.

☐ Cardigan bumped it with
his antlers.

Prove It! What evidence in the story supports your answer? Check the boxes. ☑ Make notes.

Evidence	Notes
☐ what happens in the courtroom	
☐ what the judge does and says	
☐ the illustrations	
☐	

Write About It!

CAUSE AND EFFECT

Answer question 2 using evidence from the text.

_____

_____

_____

_____

_____

_____

_____

Neighbors Working Together

1 A neighborhood can be a street. It can be more than one street. Good neighbors **figure** out ways to help one another.

Tell about a time when you had to figure out a way to do something.

_____

_____

_____

2 Some people wanted to make their neighborhood look better. They **contacted** their neighbors. They met to talk about what they could do.

How have you contacted your friends?

_____

_____

_____

22

3 Many neighbors wanted big flower pots on the street corners. The pots would cost money. Some people did not earn a lot of money. How could they pay for flower pots?

What could you do to <u>earn</u> money?

_____

_____

_____

4 The neighbors had a yard sale. Each neighbor brought things to sell. Many customers came. The neighbors made money. Now they could buy flower pots!

How could neighbors get <u>customers</u> to come to their yard sale?

_____

_____

_____

Not Just a Little!

by
Lois Grippo

Bob loved to make good things to eat. He grew wheat and vegetables on his farm. He had chickens. He used them to make yummy meals. Still, it was no fun cooking for just himself. It was no fun eating alone.

Bob wanted to share his food with his neighbors. He wanted to sit around a big table. He wanted to laugh and have fun.

Stop Think Write

UNDERSTANDING CHARACTERS

Why does Bob want to eat with his neighbors?

Bob called his neighbor Luis. "Can you come to my house for dinner?" Bob asked.

"I cannot leave the store," Luis said. "I am staying open late to earn more money."

Luis sold fruit and vegetables. He never made time to talk or have fun. Bob called his other neighbors. They were busy, too. Bob sat on his porch and thought. He tried to figure out a way to get his neighbors together.

Stop | **Think** | **Write**

VOCABULARY

How does Luis <u>earn</u> money?

_____

_____

_____

25

Bob came up with a plan. He cooked chicken in a pot. It smelled very good. Bob went to the park with his pot of chicken.

Bob walked past Luis's store. The door was open. Luis smelled the chicken. He came outside and saw Bob.

"What is making that good smell?" Luis asked.

"The smell is the chicken in my pot," said Bob.

INFER AND PREDICT

Why do you think Bob doesn't eat his chicken at home?

_____

_____

_____

"There is a picnic at four o'clock," Bob said. "You must come! You can bring some food. Tell your customers to come, too."

"I am too busy for a picnic. I have to work," said Luis. Then he smelled the chicken again. "Maybe I will close the store early. I can bring a little corn to the picnic."

"No, no! Not just a little!" said Bob. "Bring lots of corn!"

Stop Think Write

VOCABULARY

Name three things customers might buy in Luis's store.

_____

_____

_____

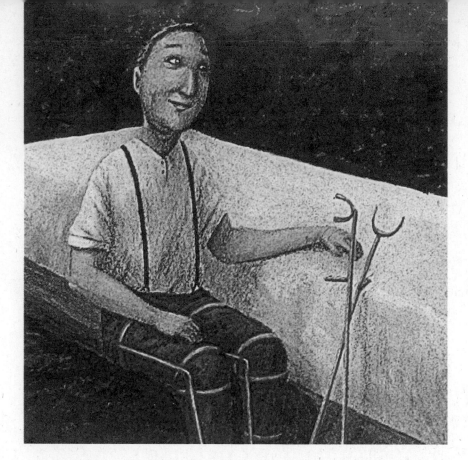

Bob went on his way. He stopped at the library. He stopped at the hardware store. Everyone smelled Bob's chicken. They all wanted to come to the picnic.

At last, Bob arrived at the park. He put his chicken on the table. Bob's neighbor Lee came by.

Stop   Think   Write

INFER AND PREDICT

Why does Bob stop at the library and the hardware store?

_____

_____

_____

28

"Luis contacted me. He told me there is a picnic. I will bring a little bit of milk," Lee said.

"No, no! Not just a little!" said Bob. "Bring lots of milk."

At four o'clock, Lee came back to the park. He brought lots of milk. Luis came to the park with lots of corn.

Stop Think Write

VOCABULARY

How might Luis have <u>contacted</u> Lee?

_____

_____

_____

More and more people came to the park. They all brought lots of food. Soon the picnic became a grand party.

Everyone had fun. Everyone talked and laughed together. Bob was happy. His plan worked just fine.

Stop **Think** **Write**

SUMMARIZE

What was Bob's plan?

_____

_____

_____

Look Back and Respond

1 **Write three things to tell about Bob.**

Hint

Look for clues on page 24.

_____

_____

_____

2 **Write two things to tell about Luis.**

Hint

Look for clues on page 25.

_____

_____

_____

3 **How are Bob and Luis alike?**

Hint

Look on pages 26 and 27. Do you think Luis likes eating tasty food?

_____

_____

_____

Be a Reading Detective!

Return to

"Destiny's Gift"
Student Book pp. 87–109

1 How does Mrs. Wade feel about Destiny at the end of the story?

☐ worried   ☐ grateful   ☐ proud

☐ other _____

Prove It! What evidence in the story supports your answer? Check the boxes. ☑ Make notes.

Evidence	Notes
☐ what Destiny says and does	
☐ what Mrs. Wade says and does	
☐ the illustrations	
☐	

Write About It!

UNDERSTANDING CHARACTERS

Answer question **1** using evidence from the text.

_____

_____

_____

_____

_____

_____

2 **Mrs. Wade might have to close her bookstore.**
Is this problem solved by the end of the story?

☐ yes   ☐ no

Prove It! What evidence in the story supports your answer? Check the boxes. ☑ Make notes.

Evidence	Notes
☐ what Destiny says and does	
☐ what Mrs. Wade says and does	
☐ what Destiny's parents say	
☐ the illustrations	

Write About It!

STORY STRUCTURE

Answer question 2 using evidence from the text.

_____

_____

_____

_____

_____

_____

_____

balancing
crew
excitement
stretch

People Working Together

A new park is about to open. It needs a nature trail. A **crew** of helpers clears the land for a path.

A creek goes across the trail. The helpers will build a bridge. It will **stretch** across the creek.

The ranger puts a log over the creek. He walks across it. He is good at **balancing** on things. He does not fall.

The helpers add more logs. They use rope to hold the logs together. Soon the bridge is done. The workers are filled with **excitement**.

1 A _____ of people can make a bridge. They work together to build it.

2 The workers are all full of

_____ when they

finish the bridge.

3 A person who is not good at

_____ might fall.

4 How can you tell when someone is full of <u>excitement</u>?

_____

_____

_____

5 Why does a bridge have to <u>stretch</u> from one side of the creek to the other?

_____

_____

_____

Building a New Barn

by Margaret Maugenest

The farmer looks at her barn. Once, the barn looked good. The wood boards were straight. The roof was strong.

Now the barn is old. The planks sag. The roof is sinking in. The paint is chipped.

The farmer is not happy. She wants to build a new barn.

Stop Think Write

COMPARE AND CONTRAST

How did the barn look when it was new? How does the barn look now?

_____

_____

_____

34

Getting Started

A **crew** of helpers comes. Some of the workers are from town. Some of them come from other farms. They are all ready to work!

First, they tear down the old barn. The workers take away the used planks.

Some people chop down nearby trees. They saw the wood into planks. The new planks will be used to build the barn.

Stop   Think   Write

VOCABULARY

How does a crew help when there are many tasks to do?

_____

_____

_____

Everyone Helps!

Some people will build the barn. There are other jobs, too. The workers will get hungry. So some people will make lunch for them.

A few workers brought their children. The children watch. They will see how a barn is built. Some day they may build a barn.

MAIN IDEAS AND DETAILS

Why doesn't everyone help build the barn?

_____

_____

_____

_____

36

The Work Begins

To begin, workers place big blocks of stone in the ground. These will make the base of the barn.

Next, the builders make a frame for each wall. They measure the wood. Then they saw it into pieces.

The pieces are joined together. The team uses nails. The nails are metal. Sometimes they use pegs. The pegs are carved from wood.

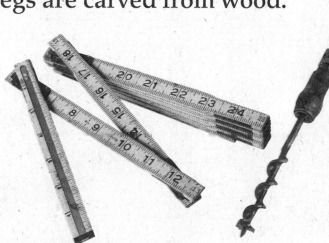

Stop   Think   Write

COMPARE AND CONTRAST

Compare nails and pegs. How are they different? How are they the same?

_____

_____

_____

Step by Step

Soon it is time to raise the barn. Workers lift the frames by hand. It is hard work. They need help. So other workers use long poles to push the frames into place.

The top comes next. Some workers climb the frame. They must be good at balancing on the frame so they do not fall off.

MAIN IDEAS AND DETAILS

Stop   Think   Write

How are the frames raised and pushed into place?

_____

_____

_____

38

The workers pull up long planks of wood. The planks **stretch** across the top of the barn. They fit into slots in the frame.

All the parts are nailed down. Now the roof will be very strong. Some barn roofs are slanted. Others are curved. This roof is curved.

Stop   Think   Write

SEQUENCE OF EVENTS

What happens after the workers fit the wood planks into the frame?

_____

_____

_____

A New Barn!

The workers stop for lunch. Then they go back to work. It is almost dark when the last nail is hammered into place. The workers feel **excitement**. They are happy and smiling. The barn is finished!

The new barn looks great. The farmer is very happy. She thanks everyone.

The workers are tired. They walk to their cars and trucks, and they go home.

VOCABULARY

Why do the workers feel <u>excitement</u>?

_____

_____

_____

Look Back and Respond

1 **Compare what the children do with what the grownups do.**

Hint

For clues, see page 36.

_____

_____

_____

2 **How does the farmer feel at the beginning of the story? How does she feel at the end? Why?**

Hint

For clues, see pages 34 and 40.

_____

_____

_____

3 **How do you think the workers on the team began learning how to build barns?**

Hint

For clues, see page 36.

_____

_____

_____

Be a Reading Detective!

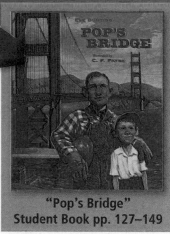

Return to

"Pop's Bridge"
Student Book pp. 127–149

1 **In what way has Robert changed at the end of the story?**

☐ He is proud of his father.

☐ He realizes that Mr. Shu's job matters.

☐ He is braver than he was.

Prove It! What evidence in the story supports your answer? Check the boxes. ☑ Make notes.

Evidence	Notes
☐ why he calls the bridge "Pop's bridge"	
☐ how he feels after the accident	
☐ what he does with the last puzzle piece	

Write About It!

COMPARE AND CONTRAST

Answer question 1 using evidence from the text.

_____

_____

_____

_____

_____

_____

_____

2 **Robert tells this story.** What detail does Robert tell readers that no other character could tell them?

- ☐ what his father's job is
- ☐ why he hid the last puzzle piece
- ☐ what people ate at the party

Prove It! What evidence in the story supports your answer? Check the boxes. ☑ Make notes.

Evidence	Notes
☐ what Robert thinks, says, and does	
☐ what Charlie says and does	
☐ the illustrations	

Write About It!

POINT OF VIEW

Answer question 2 using evidence from the text.

_____

_____

_____

_____

_____

_____

✓ **TARGET VOCABULARY**

fans
league
pronounced
stands

Baseball

1 The first baseball **league** had nine teams. They began to play each other in 1871. Today, Major League Baseball has two leagues.

In what kind of sports league would you like to play?

_____

_____

_____

2 **Fans** cheer for their favorite baseball teams. Fans go crazy when their team scores a run.

Are you and your friends fans of something? Explain.

_____

_____

_____

3 The best teams in the leagues play in the World Series. In 2011, the Texas Rangers played against the St. Louis Cardinals. An announcer pronounced the names of the players before each game.

Tell about a time someone pronounced your name wrong.

_____

_____

_____

4 People sit in the stands at baseball games. Fans can often buy drinks or food to eat while they watch the game.

What would you eat in the stands at a baseball game?

_____

_____

_____

Let's Play Ball!

by Lois Grippo

Baseball for Kids

Kids all over the United States love to play baseball. Most towns have a **league** for children. Teams play baseball in the spring and summer.

Boys and girls play on the teams. They play other teams from nearby towns. The players' friends and families watch from the **stands**.

Stop   Think   Write

VOCABULARY

How is a league different from a team?

_____

_____

_____

44

The Beginning of Little League

Baseball leagues for kids did not always exist. A man named Carl Stotz started the Little League about 70 years ago. Carl loved baseball. He thought baseball was good for kids. It was a great way to teach teamwork.

Carl's neighbors thought so, too. They raised $35 to start three teams. They got stores to donate uniforms. Carl called it the Little League.

Stop   Think   Write

CAUSE AND EFFECT

How did Carl's neighbors help start the Little League?

_____

_____

_____

Little League Then and Now

The very first Little League game was played on June 6, 1939. The Lundy Lumber team played against the Lycoming Dairy team. Lundy Lumber won.

Today, Little League teams play in every state. They play in 80 countries, too. Little League is the biggest organized sports program in the world.

Do you think Little League is more popular now than in 1939? Explain.

_____

_____

_____

Learning Skills

Baseball players learn many skills. They must hit the ball with the bat. They must run fast around the bases. Players need to catch balls. They have to tag runners and throw the ball to other players.

One player can't win a game alone. Kids learn to work as a team. They practice, and they get better. They learn to count on each other.

Stop Think Write

CAUSE AND EFFECT

When players practice as a team, what are some ways they improve?

_____

_____

_____

Going to the Big Leagues

Some great baseball players got started in Little League. One of them was Cal Ripken, Jr. He played for the Baltimore Orioles.

Baltimore fans loved Ripken. They cheered when the announcer pronounced his name. Ripken played in 2,632 straight games! He is in the Baseball Hall of Fame.

Stop Think Write

How did <u>fans</u> show that they loved Cal Ripken?

_____

_____

_____

Life After Little League

Many Little League players do not become great baseball players. Some go on to do other important work. Krissy Wendell became a great hockey player. Her team won a silver medal in the Olympics.

Little League teaches teamwork skills. People can use these skills all their lives. Little League players can become teachers, firefighters, nurses, and engineers. They can do any job working with other people.

Stop   Think   Write

CONCLUSIONS

Tell about a job in which it is important for people to work as a team. Explain.

_____

_____

_____

49

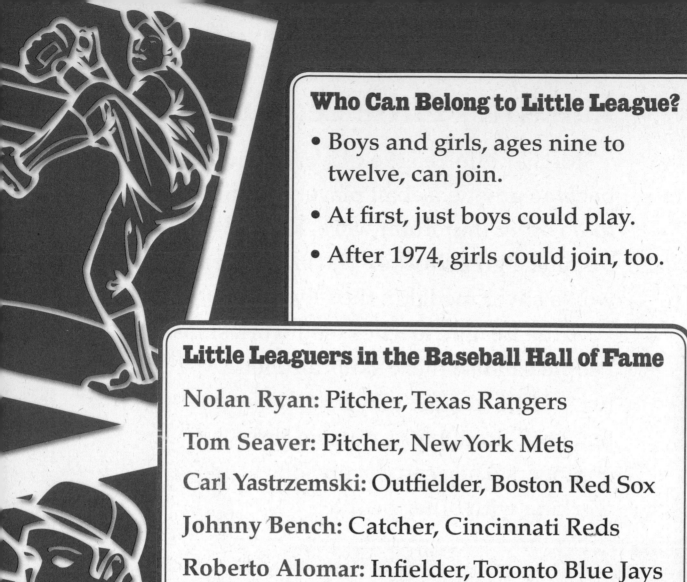

Who Can Belong to Little League?

- Boys and girls, ages nine to twelve, can join.

- At first, just boys could play.

- After 1974, girls could join, too.

Little Leaguers in the Baseball Hall of Fame

Nolan Ryan: Pitcher, Texas Rangers

Tom Seaver: Pitcher, New York Mets

Carl Yastrzemski: Outfielder, Boston Red Sox

Johnny Bench: Catcher, Cincinnati Reds

Roberto Alomar: Infielder, Toronto Blue Jays

Stop   Think   Write

INFER AND PREDICT

What do you think a player must do to be in the Baseball Hall of Fame?

_____

_____

_____

Look Back and Respond

1 How do you think <u>fans</u> affect the way teams play baseball?

_____

_____

_____

Hint
Think about how you feel when people cheer you on.

2 Why did Carl Stotz think baseball was good for kids?

_____

_____

_____

Hint
For a clue, look on page 45.

3 How can you tell that Carl's neighbors thought Little League was a good idea?

_____

_____

_____

Hint
Look on page 45.

Be a Reading Detective!

Return to

"Roberto Clemente"
Student Book pp. 167–189

1 **Why did Roberto Clemente first come to Pittsburgh?**

☐ He was asked to join the Pirates.

☐ The Pirates were a winning team.

☐ He was well known in the United States.

Prove It! What evidence in the selection supports your answer? Check the boxes. ☑ Make notes.

Evidence	Notes
☐ details about Clemente's childhood	
☐ details about his early career	
☐ details about the Pittsburgh Pirates	

Write About It!

CAUSE AND EFFECT

Answer question 1 using evidence from the text.

_____

_____

_____

_____

_____

_____

_____

51A

2 **What was the author's main purpose for writing?**

☐ to tell a life story

☐ to tell about baseball

☐ to persuade readers to watch baseball games

Prove It! What evidence in the selection supports your answer? Check the boxes. ☑ Make notes.

Evidence	Notes
☐ Clemente's words and actions	
☐ dates and place names	
☐ what others said about Clemente	

Write About It!

AUTHOR'S PURPOSE

Answer question ❷ using evidence from the text.

_____

_____

_____

_____

_____

_____

_____

Night Animals

Bats are not the only animals that are active at night.

An owl **swoops** through the darkness looking for food. It feeds on other animals that are out at night. The owl might catch a small snake as it **slithers** across the ground. The snake **dozes** during the day.

Most night animals have strong eyes and good hearing. They can hunt well at night. They are safer, too.

You can find hedgehogs, raccoons, and foxes up at night. The **squeak** of a house mouse lets you know that it is up at night, too.

1 When a snake moves, it

_____, because

it has no legs.

2 If you hear a

_____, it might

be a cat's toy, an old chair, or a mouse.

3 Someone who

_____ in class

will not learn very much!

4 What can you tell about an animal
that <u>swoops</u>?

_____

_____

_____

_____

Owls

by Linda Vasquez

There are about 200 kinds of owls around the world. Some of them are big. Some are small. The biggest owl in North America is the great gray owl. It can be almost three feet long. The smallest owl is probably the elf owl. It is about as heavy as a slice of bread.

Owls feed on small mammals, insects, birds, and snakes. They can catch an animal that flies, runs, or slithers. Some owls even catch fish. Most owls hunt at night.

Stop Think Write

COMPARE AND CONTRAST

How are the great gray owl and the elf owl the same? How are they different?

_____

_____

_____

Hunting

There are a few reasons that owls hunt at night. They can see better at night than most other animals. They can also hear better. Their color makes them hard to see in the dark.

An owl may wait on a perch until it hears or sees a small animal. When an owl flies, it is silent. A small animal cannot hear the owl as it swoops down.

Stop Think Write

SEQUENCE OF EVENTS

What does an owl do after it sees a small animal?

Sight

Owls have very big eyes. This helps them see in the dark. Most birds have eyes on the sides of their heads, but owls have eyes in the front. They can see exactly how far away an animal is.

An owl cannot move its eyes. Instead, it moves its head. It can move its head to look backward, even while it is flying.

Stop   Think   Write

MAIN IDEA AND DETAILS

What are some unusual things about an owl's eyes?

_____

_____

_____

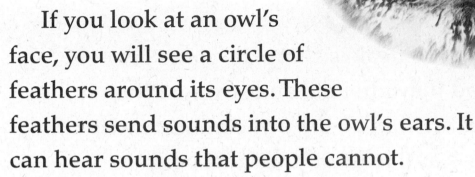

Hearing

If you look at an owl's face, you will see a circle of feathers around its eyes. These feathers send sounds into the owl's ears. It can hear sounds that people cannot.

Some owls' ears are at different places on each side of the head. They hear a sound in one ear a little sooner than in the other ear. This helps them know where an animal is. They use their ears the way we use our eyes!

Stop   Think   Write

CAUSE AND EFFECT

How can an owl pinpoint where its prey is?

_____

_____

_____

Feeding

An owl's beak is sharp. Its claws are, too, and they are long and strong. When it catches an animal, the owl crushes it with its claws and tears at it with its beak.

It swallows the animal whole. Later, it spits up a pellet with the fur and bones that remain.

Stop Think Write

SEQUENCE OF EVENTS

What does an owl do after it catches an animal?

_____

_____

_____

Owlets

Owls do not build their nests. They may live in an old nest that another bird made. They may live in holes in trees, in ditches, or on ledges of buildings.

Baby owls are called owlets. The eggs do not hatch at the same time, so the owlets in a family may be different sizes. Owlets get very hungry. If there are owlets near you, you might hear them squeak all night as they ask for food.

Stop Think Write

VOCABULARY

What might it mean when an owlet makes a squeak?

_____

_____

_____

Who Gives a Hoot?

While the neighborhood dozes, owls are busy. You may have heard one hoot during the night. Or maybe you have heard an owl screech, or even whistle.

In the past, some people thought owls were very wise. Other people thought that they brought bad luck.

People today still find owls mysterious. But one thing we know for sure is that owls help get rid of pests.

Stop **Think** **Write**

CONCLUSIONS

Why do people find owls mysterious?

_____

_____

_____

Look Back and Respond

1 Write in order the events that happen when an owl goes hunting.

For clues, see pages 55 and 58.

_____

_____

_____

2 Why might young owls in the same family be different sizes?

For a clue, see page 59.

_____

_____

_____

3 What kinds of noises do owls make?

For clues, see pages 59 and 60.

_____

_____

_____

Be a Reading Detective!

1 What happens after Bat eats the moth?

☐ She sneezes.　　☐ She shouts.

☐ She listens hard.

"Bat Loves the Night"
Student Book pp. 211–225

Prove It! What evidence in the selection supports your answer? Check the boxes. ☑ Make notes.

Evidence	Notes
☐ how Bat uses her hearing	
☐ the text about the events	
☐ the illustrations	
☐	

Write About It!

SEQUENCE OF EVENTS

Answer question **1** using evidence from the text.

_____

_____

_____

_____

_____

_____

_____

2 **Why does Bat go back to her home?**

☐ She needs to find food.

☐ She does not feel well.

☐ Daylight is coming.

Prove It! What evidence in the selection supports your answer? Check the boxes. ☑ Make notes.

Evidence	Notes
☐ how Bat gets her food	
☐ details about day and night	
☐ when Bat wakes and sleeps	
☐ the illustrations	

Write About It!

CAUSE AND EFFECT

Answer question ② using evidence from the text.

_____

_____

_____

_____

_____

_____

_____

**illustrate
imagine
sketches
tools**

Words and Pictures in Books

Check the answer.

1 An artist can _____ a story with pictures. The pictures help you understand the story.

☐ **illustrate** ☐ **murmur** ☐ **cling**

2 An artist can draw something from real life. An artist can _____ something to draw, too. Then the artist will draw a made-up picture.

☐ **raise** ☐ **stretch** ☐ **imagine**

3 Some artists make quick drawings first. These _____ may not show a lot of details.

☐ **customers** ☐ **sketches** ☐ **tools**

4 What are some drawing <u>tools</u> you might have at home?

_____

_____

_____

5 How would you <u>illustrate</u> a story about trees?

_____

_____

_____

Caw Caw

Douglas Florian's Books

by Gail Mack

The Boy Who Loved Drawing

Douglas Florian wasn't the first artist in his family. His dad was.

Douglas's dad loved to make sketches of things in nature. He showed Douglas how to draw. He taught Douglas how to look closely at nature.

Stop   Think   Write

INFER AND PREDICT

What things in nature can someone draw or paint?

_____

_____

_____

64

Drawing was fun for Douglas. When he was ten years old, he entered a coloring contest. His art won second place. His prize was a pair of roller skates.

Stop   Think   Write

CAUSE AND EFFECT

Why did Douglas win a prize?

_____

_____

_____

An Art Student

One summer, Douglas took an art class. He loved it. He learned to use different art **tools**. Artists use many tools. They might use paint or pen and ink. They might even use chalk.

Douglas was just fifteen years old. He already knew what he wanted to become. He was going to be an artist.

Stop · Think · Write

What kinds of tools might an artist use?

_____

_____

_____

A Working Artist

Douglas did become an artist. He sold his drawings to magazines and newspapers. He made art for children's books, too.

At first, he would **illustrate** other people's stories. Later, he wrote his own stories. His first books were about nature. Douglas filled them with drawings of things like frogs, turtles, and shells.

Stop **Think** **Write**

VOCABULARY

What do people do when they <u>illustrate</u> a story?

_____

_____

_____

A Writer of Poems

One day, Douglas saw a book of silly poems. He smiled as he turned the pages. "A book like this would be fun to make!" he thought.

So he wrote some poems. He used funny sounds and silly words. He made enough poems to fill a book. Then he drew pictures for the poems.

Stop   Think   Write

TEXT AND GRAPHIC FEATURES

How does the picture show a funny sound?

_____

_____

_____

Poetry Award

A Winner

Douglas liked to imagine made-up animals. He wrote a book of poems about them. After that, he wrote a book of poems about real animals. It was called *Beast Feast*. His books were a big hit. One book even won an award!

Douglas still loves making art and writing poems. His books make kids laugh.

Stop   Think   Write

TEXT AND GRAPHIC FEATURES

What detail in the text does the picture of Douglas Florian show?

_____

_____

_____

69

Douglas Florian Timeline

This timeline shows events in Douglas Florian's life.

1950	Douglas Florian is born.
1960	He wins second prize in an art contest.
1965	He decides to become an artist.
Around 1970	He studies art in college.
1994	His poem book, *Beast Feast*, comes out.
1995	*Beast Feast* wins the Lee Bennett Hopkins Poetry Award.

Stop Think Write

TEXT AND GRAPHIC FEATURES

What is one event on the timeline that you don't read about anywhere else in this story?

_____

_____

_____

Look Back and Respond

1 What did Douglas Florian do after he made pictures for other people's stories?

Hint

Look on page 67.

_____

_____

_____

2 How did Douglas Florian's dad help him become an artist?

Hint

Look on page 64.

_____

_____

_____

3 Write three words that tell about Douglas Florian's art. Explain.

Hint

Clues are on almost every page!

_____

_____

_____

"What Do Illustrators Do?"
Student Book pp. 243–261

Be a Reading Detective!

1 What two things does an illustrator's dummy show?

☐ the size and shape of the book

☐ sketches of the pictures

☐ the whole plan on one page

Prove It! What evidence in the selection supports your answer? Check the boxes. ☑ Make notes.

Evidence	Notes
☐ the text	
☐ cartoons with speech balloons	
☐ other illustrations	

Write About It!

TEXT AND GRAPHIC FEATURES

Answer question 1 using evidence from the text.

_____

_____

_____

_____

_____

_____

_____

2 **What is the same in both illustrators' stories?**

☐ The main character is a girl.

☐ A beanstalk grows high in the sky.

☐ The illustrator's pet is in the story.

Prove It! What evidence in the selection supports your answer? Check the boxes. ☑ Make notes.

Evidence	Notes
☐ the text	
☐ cartoons with speech balloons	
☐ other illustrations	

Write About It!

COMPARE AND CONTRAST

Answer question 2 using evidence from the text.

_____

_____

_____

_____

_____

_____

_____

✓ TARGET VOCABULARY

advice
ashamed
harvest
serious

Planting a Garden

It was time to plant my garden. My friends gave lots of advice. They said I should plant corn, lettuce, and squash.

I planted only beans. "You are so serious about beans!" my friend Yolanda said. "Why only beans?"

Do you want to know the truth? I hadn't looked carefully at the seed packs. I was ashamed to admit my mistake. "I like beans," I said. "I like them a lot!"

I went to work. I weeded and watered. I had a good harvest. I ate beans for a month. Next year, I don't think I'll plant any beans.

1. People like to give _____ that they think will help you.

2. During a _____, you gather crops that have grown.

3. If you are _____ about gardening, you work hard to make your garden grow.

4. Write a word that means the opposite of <u>ashamed</u>.

   _____

5. Tell about a time when someone gave you <u>advice</u>.

   _____

   _____

   _____

Living Things Are Linked

A Retelling of an African Tale

by Dina McClellan

Once there was a chief who was a stern ruler. He demanded that all in the village obey him. Anyone who did not was punished terribly.

Only one person was not afraid of the chief. That was his grandmother. Who knows why the chief did not punish her. Maybe he just didn't take notice of her.

Stop Think Write

CONCLUSIONS

How can you tell the chief is a stern ruler?

_____

_____

_____

One night the chief couldn't sleep. The frogs outside were making too much noise. This was a serious problem for the chief.

He woke up all the people in the village. "If I can't sleep, no one will sleep," he said. "Kill all the frogs!"

Stop **Think** **Write**

CAUSE AND EFFECT

Why can't the chief sleep?

_____

_____

_____

So the people killed all the frogs. Later they felt ashamed. They did not like what they had done. They were all afraid of the chief.

Only the chief's grandmother was not afraid. "You'll be sorry," she said. "All living things are linked. Even you and the frogs."

The chief had to laugh. "How could frogs be linked to a big chief like me?" he said.

Stop Think Write

Why do you think people feel <u>ashamed</u> of killing the frogs?

_____

_____

_____

Soon it was time for the harvest. Everyone in the village had to gather beans and sweet potatoes. It was hard to work outdoors. The air was full of mosquitoes. Thousands of them!

The chief stayed in his hut while others worked. The mosquitoes found him there. He couldn't sleep or think. There was too much buzzing! The chief was covered with bites.

Stop   Think   Write

VOCABULARY

What happens during a <u>harvest</u>?

_____

_____

_____

"Kill the mosquitoes!" the chief said. "I want every last one killed by morning!"

"Why didn't you take my advice?" said the grandmother. "We are in this mess because you killed the frogs."

The chief paid no attention to her. Again he told the villagers to kill the mosquitoes.

CONCLUSIONS

Stop Think Write

How do you think people feel about killing the mosquitoes? Why?

_____

_____

_____

_____

People did their best. Still, they couldn't kill every mosquito. There were too many. The next day there were even more.

The chief gave another order. "This time, kill them ALL!" he said.

The people tried again. They did their best. They still couldn't kill all the mosquitoes. There were just too many.

Stop **Think** **Write**

UNDERSTANDING CHARACTERS

How do you think the chief feels when he sees that there are more mosquitoes than ever?

_____

_____

_____

"You should have left those frogs alone," said the grandmother.

"What are you talking about?" said the chief. He was very angry.

"Don't you know that frogs eat mosquitoes? That's why you need frogs!" the grandmother said.

At last, the chief learned his lesson. He found out the hard way that all living things are linked.

Stop Think Write

INFER AND PREDICT

How do frogs help people?

_____

_____

_____

Look Back and Respond

1 Is the chief a good listener? How can you tell?

Hint

For clues, look on pages 74, 76, and 78.

_____

_____

_____

2 Why do the people do whatever the chief tells them to do?

Hint

For clues, look on pages 74 and 76.

_____

_____

_____

3 How is the chief's grandmother unlike the other characters in the story?

Hint

For clues, look on pages 74 and 76.

_____

_____

_____

Be a Reading Detective!

Return to

THE HARVEST BIRDS

"The Harvest Birds"
Student Book pp. 279–297

1 **What two actions show that Juan is determined to become a farmer?**

☐ He works in the shops in town.

☐ He begs Grandpa Chon for some land.

☐ He sweeps the floor to get seeds for his field.

Prove It! What evidence in the story supports your answer? Check the boxes. ☑ Make notes.

Evidence	Notes
☐ what Juan says and does	
☐ what other characters say	
☐ the illustrations	

Write About It!

CONCLUSIONS

Answer question 1 using evidence from the text.

_____

_____

_____

_____

_____

_____

2 **Which characters help Juan get and use his land?**

☐ Don Tobias

☐ Grandpa Chon

☐ the birds

Prove It! What evidence in the story supports your answer? Check the boxes. ☑ Make notes.

Evidence	Notes
☐ what Juan says and does	
☐ what other characters say and do	
☐ the illustrations	

Write About It!

STORY STRUCTURE

Answer question 2 using evidence from the text.

_____

_____

_____

_____

_____

_____

_____

applause
familiar
jerky
vacant

Storytelling

1 Children in France made a discovery about one hundred years ago. They were in a vacant cave. They found pictures on the rock walls. The cave paintings were thousands of years old. The pictures told the story of people who lived there long ago.

What other things can be <u>vacant</u>?

_____

_____

_____

2 In the past, storytellers went from town to town. They shared their stories. Some familiar stories were first told long ago.

How do you become <u>familiar</u> with something?

_____

_____

_____

3 Storytellers of long ago were fun to watch. Some wore colorful clothes. They sometimes acted out their stories. They made jerky movements and funny faces.

What is a word that means the opposite of jerky?

_____

4 Long ago, good storytellers got lots of applause. People clap when they hear good stories today, too!

When do we hear applause?

_____

_____

_____

Puppets Around the World

by Lois Grippo

People love puppets! They are a familiar toy. Children all around the world love to play with them.

The first puppets may have been made in Egypt. These puppets were simple toys. They were made of wood. Strings made their parts move.

Stop Think Write

MAIN IDEAS AND DETAILS

What were puppets like long ago in Egypt?

_____

_____

_____

84

Shadow Puppets

Long ago, people in Southeast Asia made shadow puppets. These puppets were flat. They were made from paper. Each puppet was attached to a stick. Moving the stick made the puppet move.

The puppets were held behind a silk screen. Candles were lit to make shadows.

People sat on the other side of the screen. They could not see the puppets. They could not see the people holding them. They saw large puppet shadows on the silk screen!

Stop Think Write

CAUSE AND EFFECT

How does a shadow puppet move?

_____

_____

_____

Bunraku Puppets

The Japanese also make special puppets. They are called Bunraku puppets. These puppets are large. They can be as big as a person.

It takes three people to move these puppets. The people appear on stage with the puppet.

The puppet's movements are never jerky. People work hard to make the puppets move smoothly.

Stop   Think   Write

Why aren't the movements of a Bunraku puppet <u>jerky</u>?

_____

_____

_____

Hand Puppets

Did you ever make a sock puppet?
A sock puppet is a hand puppet.

There were hand puppets long ago in
China. These puppets were not made
from socks. They were made from wood.
The wood was hollow. A person's hand
fit inside.

Stop Think Write

CAUSE AND EFFECT

How does a hand puppet move?

_____

_____

_____

Puppet Theaters

Puppet shows are done on small stages. Sometimes the stage is vacant. Often it is filled. There may be trees and homes. There may be hills and farms.

Puppets race across the stage. They peek out of windows. Fans give applause when a hero fights a dragon. They boo when the dragon fights back. Puppet shows are fun.

VOCABULARY

Why might you hear <u>applause</u> during a puppet show?

_____

_____

_____

Puppet Shows

What are puppet shows about? Some teach a lesson. Some tell the history of a place. Long ago there were no TVs. There were no newspapers. People learned the news from puppet shows.

So listen closely to puppets! They can be very funny. They can also tell you things you did not know!

Stop | Think | Write

MAIN IDEAS AND DETAILS

What can you learn from a puppet show?

_____

_____

_____

89

Make a Sock Puppet

✳ Ask a grown-up to give you an old sock.

✳ Draw a face on the foot part of the sock.

✳ Now, stick your hand in the sock.

✳ Use your fingers to make a mouth.

✳ Move the mouth up and down.

✳ Make your sock say something!

Stop   Think   Write

MAIN IDEAS AND DETAILS

How do you make the mouth of a sock puppet?

Look Back and Respond

1 How do people make Bunraku puppets move in lifelike ways?

Hint
For clues, see page 86.

_____

_____

_____

2 How do you think stage scenery helps to bring a puppet show to life?

Hint
For clues, see page 88.

_____

_____

_____

3 What is the difference between a Bunraku puppet and a shadow puppet?

Hint
For clues, see pages 85 and 86.

_____

_____

_____

Be a Reading Detective!

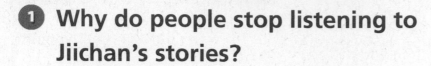

"Kamishibai Man"
Student Book pp. 319–341

1 Why do people stop listening to Jiichan's stories?

☐ He is too old to tell them well.

☐ The children want to watch TV.

☐ He tells his stories on TV.

Prove It! What evidence in the selection supports your answer? Check the boxes. ☑ Make notes.

Evidence	Notes
☐ what Jiichan says and does	
☐ what other characters say and do	
☐ details about television	

Write About It!

CAUSE AND EFFECT

Answer question **1** using evidence from the text.

_____

_____

_____

_____

_____

_____

_____

2 **Which event happens earliest?**

☐ Jiichan sees very tall buildings.

☐ Jiichan often tells stories to children.

☐ Jiichan sees that trees have been chopped down.

Prove It! What evidence in the selection supports your answer? Check the boxes. ☑ Make notes.

Evidence	Notes
☐ what Jiichan says	
☐ what people say about Jiichan	
☐ words like "in the old days"	
☐ how old Jiichan looks in different illustrations	

Write About It!

SEQUENCE OF EVENTS

Answer question 2 using evidence from the text.

_____

_____

_____

_____

_____

_____

_____

experiment
genius
invention
laboratory

Inventors

① An inventor starts with an idea. The inventor does an **experiment** to see if the idea will work.

What experiment could you do to find out which kind of cereal stays crunchy in milk the longest?

_____

_____

_____

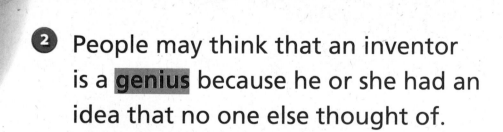

② People may think that an inventor is a **genius** because he or she had an idea that no one else thought of.

What else could someone do that would make you think that person is a genius?

_____

_____

_____

3 If an **invention** is useful, lots of people will want it. The inventor may become famous.

What kind of _invention_ would you like to make?

_____

_____

_____

4 An inventor often works in a **laboratory**. It has equipment to make and test inventions.

What are three things you might find in a _laboratory_?

_____

_____

_____

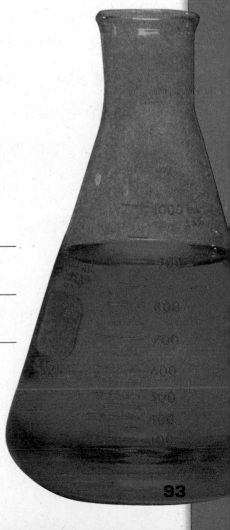

Aleck's **Big** Ideas

by Candyce Norvell

Inventions and Inventors

Think of great inventions of the last one hundred years. The telephone, television, car, and computer are a few of them.

We know how amazing these things are. What about the people who made them? An inventor can be as amazing as his or her invention. This is the story of one amazing inventor.

Stop Think Write

CONCLUSIONS

Why were the telephone and the car amazing inventions?

_____

_____

_____

A Boy Named Aleck

In 1847, a boy named Aleck was born in Scotland. He became interested in sound.

One day Aleck got lost. He heard his father calling him from far away. This made Aleck curious about how sound traveled.

As a joke, Aleck and his brothers made a machine. It sounded like a baby crying. Their neighbors thought it was a real baby!

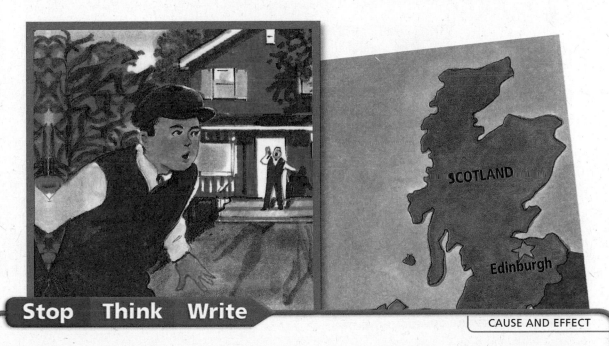

Stop **Think** **Write**

CAUSE AND EFFECT

What made Aleck think about how sound traveled?

Early Experiments

Aleck tried new experiments. He even taught his dog to talk! He rubbed its voice box. He moved its jaws. The sounds that came out were like words. Soon the dog could say, "How are you, grandmamma?"

When Aleck was 14, he made a useful machine. Until then, farmers had to take the shell off wheat. Only then could people eat it. The young genius made a machine that did this job.

Stop | Think | Write

VOCABULARY

Why do you think the author calls Aleck a genius?

_____

_____

_____

96

Growing Up

Aleck's mother was deaf. Aleck wanted to help her understand the things he said. He wanted to help people who could not hear well.

Aleck went to England to study. He met scientists there. He learned about a new idea called electricity.

Stop **Think** **Write**

MAIN IDEAS AND DETAILS

Write a detail that explains why Aleck wanted to help people who couldn't hear well.

_____

_____

_____

Off to America

Later, Aleck moved to the United States. He finished his studies. He then became a teacher. Aleck married Mabel Hubbard. Like Aleck's mother, Mabel could not hear.

Aleck began to work on his biggest invention. It was the telephone. Yes, Aleck was Alexander Graham Bell!

Stop   Think   Write

SEQUENCE OF EVENTS

What was Aleck's first job after he finished school?

_____

_____

_____

Sending a Message

Aleck had an idea. He wanted to send voice messages over a wire. He and his friend Tom Watson began to try. They worked long hours in their laboratory.

During one experiment, Aleck hurt himself. Tom was in another room. Aleck said, "Mr. Watson, come here." Tom heard Aleck's voice over the wire! The first telephone message had been sent.

Stop **Think** **Write**

VOCABULARY

What did Aleck and Tom try to do in their laboratory?

_____

_____

_____

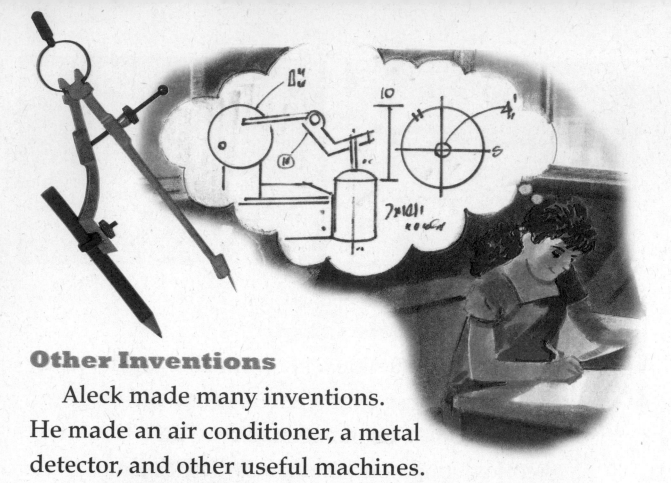

Other Inventions

Aleck made many inventions. He made an air conditioner, a metal detector, and other useful machines.

Alexander Graham Bell once said, "All really big discoveries are the results of thought." Aleck must have thought a lot. He sure made some big discoveries. Every day, other people's thoughts lead to discoveries, too.

Stop Think Write

CAUSE AND EFFECT

How can thoughts lead to big discoveries?

_____

_____

_____

Look Back and Respond

1 **What is the main idea of this story?**

Hint
Think about what every page of the story is mainly about.

_____

_____

_____

2 **Write two details that tell why Aleck was curious about sound.**

Hint
For clues, see pages 95 and 97.

_____

_____

_____

3 **How would you describe Aleck?**

Hint
For clues, see pages 95, 96, and 97.

_____

_____

_____

Be a Reading Detective!

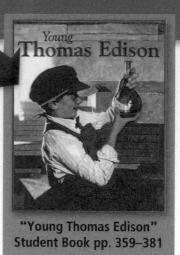

Return to

"Young Thomas Edison"
Student Book pp. 359–381

1 Which is the most important thing to know about Thomas Edison?

☐ He learned Morse code.

☐ He made useful inventions.

☐ He could not hear very well.

Prove It! What evidence in the selection supports your answer? Check the boxes. ☑ Make notes.

Evidence	Notes
☐ details about Edison's boyhood	
☐ details about Edison's jobs	
☐ details about Edison's laboratories	

Write About It!

MAIN IDEAS AND DETAILS

Answer question **1** using evidence from the text.

_____

_____

_____

_____

_____

_____

2 **How did Edison's mother influence his life?**

☐ She showed him how to mix chemicals.

☐ She got him a job as a paperboy.

☐ She taught him to ask questions.

Prove It! What evidence in the selection supports your answer? Check the boxes. ☑ Make notes.

Evidence	Notes
☐ details about Edison's childhood	
☐ details about Edison's work	
☐	

Write About It!

CAUSE AND EFFECT

Answer question 2 using evidence from the text.

_____

_____

_____

_____

_____

_____

_____

✓ **TARGET VOCABULARY**

athletes
compete
fraction
improve

ATHLETES

1 It takes skill to be the best in a sport. It takes hard work, too. Top athletes practice every day.

Which athletes do you think have to work the hardest?

_____

_____

_____

2 Many athletes like to compete. They really want to win!

In what kinds of things do you like to compete?

_____

_____

_____

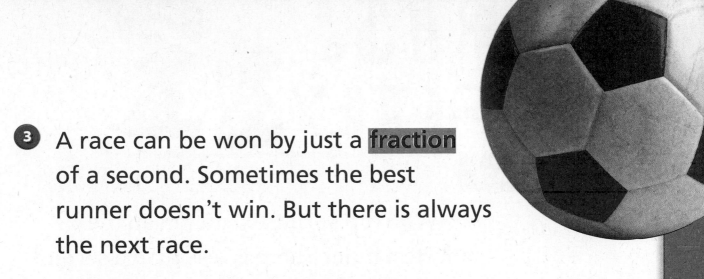

3 A race can be won by just a fraction of a second. Sometimes the best runner doesn't win. But there is always the next race.

What things can you think of that happen in a fraction of a second?

_____

_____

_____

4 If an athlete wants to stay on top, he or she must always improve. There are always other athletes who are trying to do better.

What do you enjoy doing that you would like to improve at? What can you do to get better?

_____

_____

_____

SPORTS, EXACTLY

BY CARL BROWN

Who can sprint 100 meters in the shortest time? There is less than a second between the world's best times.

Who can throw the farthest? The difference between two excellent shot-put throws can be less than one inch.

Here's another question. How do people measure such exact amounts?

Stop Think Write

MAKE INFERENCES

When sprinters race, does one person usually win by many seconds? Explain.

_____

_____

_____

TIME

The first stopwatch for sports was invented in 1869. It could measure a **fraction** of a second. By the 1960s, new watches could measure times to one hundredth of a second.

Today, computers measure sports times to one thousandth of a second. That's how we can be sure who is the world's fastest sprinter!

Stop Think Write

VOCABULARY

Why is it important in sports to measure to a fraction of a second?

_____

_____

_____

PHOTOS

It can be very hard to see who wins a close race. That's why people began to use cameras. A photo can show who crossed the finish line first.

It once took a few minutes to develop the film. People needed to **improve** the cameras. Now, digital photos are used. The cameras take 3,000 photos a second.

Stop Think Write

CAUSE AND EFFECT

Why might it be hard to see who wins a close race?

INSTANT REPLAY

Before the 1960s, football games on television were not very popular. It was hard to see what happened on the field. That was before "instant replay."

Instant replay uses video cameras to record a game. Now, after an important play, viewers can immediately see it again. They can watch the play up close and in slow motion. People watching on television have the best seats in the house!

Stop Think Write

SEQUENCE OF EVENTS

When do television viewers see an instant replay?

_____

_____

_____

BASEBALL AND TENNIS

Instant replay is also used to help the referee or umpire make good decisions. It can show if a baseball hit is a home run or a foul.

In tennis, the player has to hit the ball so that it lands inside the lines. The ball can go so fast that the athletes may not agree. Several cameras linked with a computer can show exactly where a ball hits the ground.

Stop Think Write

MAKE INFERENCES

What might cause tennis players to argue on the court?

_____

_____

_____

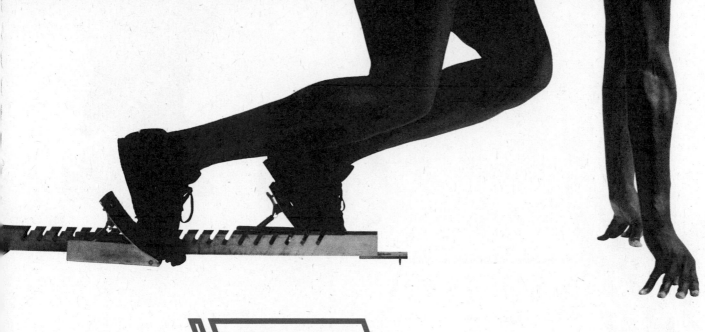

RACES

Foot races use instant replay, too. If a runner leaves the blocks less than eleven hundredths of a second after the starting gun, it's a false start. The runner must have decided to go before hearing the gun. Nobody can respond that fast!

Stop   Think   Write

MAKE INFERENCES

What would happen if a runner left the blocks before the starting gun was fired?

_____

_____

_____

SOCCER

You have read how computers and cameras help people make decisions about sports. But sometimes referees don't want to compete with machines.

Soccer games on television use instant replay. But the people who make the rules for soccer decided not to use instant replay on the field. They agree that the camera may show that a referee was right or wrong. However, they insist that a person, not a machine, should make the call.

Stop Think Write

VOCABULARY

In what way could a machine **compete** with a referee in soccer?

_____

_____

_____

Look Back and Respond

1 Which happened first: people using a stopwatch to time sports, or people using instant replay?

Hint

For clues, see pages 105 and 107.

_____

_____

_____

2 Why don't soccer referees use instant replay?

Hint

For a clue, see page 110.

_____

_____

_____

3 Why are digital cameras more useful than film cameras in sports?

Hint

For a clue, see page 106.

_____

_____

_____

Be a Reading Detective!

Return to

"Technology Wins the Game"
Student Book pp. 403–413

1 In the history of running shoes, which event came first?

☐ Running shoes had rubber soles.

☐ Runners wore sandals.

☐ People added spikes to running shoes.

Prove It! What evidence in the selection supports your answer? Check the boxes. ☑ Make notes.

Evidence	Notes
☐ the order of events in the text	
☐ time words such as *next* and *in the 1920s*	
☐ the timeline	

Write About It!

SEQUENCE OF EVENTS

Answer question **1** using evidence from the text.

_____

_____

_____

_____

_____

_____

_____

2 **What has caused runners to run faster now than they did years ago? (Check all that are true.)**

☐ tracks with all-weather surfaces

☐ clothing that fits tightly

☐ improved running shoes

Prove It! What evidence in the selection supports your answer? Check the boxes. ☑ Make notes.

Evidence	Notes
☐ details about track surfaces	
☐ details about running clothes	
☐ details about running shoes	

Write About It!

CAUSE AND EFFECT

Answer question ② using evidence from the text.

_____

_____

_____

_____

_____

_____

_____

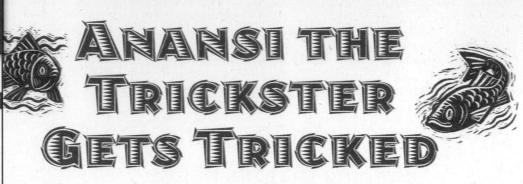

ANANSI THE TRICKSTER GETS TRICKED

Oh, that Anansi the Spider! How he hated to work!

Once, Anansi wanted fish for dinner. So he hollered for Bonsu the Tiger. No one was more foolish and trusting than Bonsu.

"We'll share the work," Anansi promised Bonsu. "You fish. I'll wait here."

Bonsu scowled. Dealing with Anansi was always a risky business.

"The worst part of any job is the tiredness that results," said Bonsu. "Do you agree?" He tugged his ear and scratched his side against a tree, trying to look at ease.

Anansi agreed with him.

"Okay!" said Bonsu. "I'll do the hard work of feeling tired. You can do the easier work of catching the fish. How's that?"

Poor Anansi! Beaten at his own game!

1. Anansi _____ loudly for Bonsu, so that he could be heard calling.

2. Bonsu _____, thinking about the unfairness of it all.

3. Doing business with a trickster is always a _____ thing.

4. What kinds of vegetables need to be <u>tugged</u> from the ground?

_____

_____

_____

ANANSI'S BAD HAIR DAY

by Dina McClellan

Anansi the Spider was once a very handsome fellow. He had a beautiful head of thick, glossy hair.

But he was very lazy. If it was up to him, he'd lounge around in his web all day while his wife worked picking corn.

"I'm tired of doing all the work around here," Anansi's wife said to him one day. "Why don't you pick corn for a change? Besides, I'm making bean stew."

Stop   Think   Write

THEME

Think about the story details on this page. What lesson might this story teach?

_____

_____

_____

Anansi sniffed. The stew smelled divine. "I can't work when I'm hungry," he sulked. Nevertheless, he grabbed his hat and started out.

The path was hot and dusty. Only the thought of his wife's delicious bean stew kept him going.

By the time he got to the field, though, all he could think about was the stew simmering in the pot. He turned and ran back home.

Stop **Think** **Write**

CAUSE AND EFFECT

What makes Anansi run back home?

_____

_____

_____

"When do we eat?" Anansi hollered as he came into the kitchen.

"When you finish picking the corn." Anansi's wife scowled.

Anansi sighed. He returned to the field. He started working. But soon enough the delicious smell of the stew drifted across the field.

Stop   Think   Write

What does the word <u>hollered</u> tell you about Anansi?

_____

_____

_____

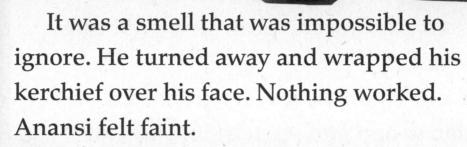

It was a smell that was impossible to ignore. He turned away and wrapped his kerchief over his face. Nothing worked. Anansi felt faint.

Just then, he spotted his wife across the field. She was carrying a bowl.

"At last!" cried Anansi, sprinting across the field toward her. He grabbed the bowl and gulped from it greedily.

"*Yecccch!*" Anansi cried, spitting it out. "But this is just water! Where's the stew?"

"Not ready yet. It will be done when you are," snapped Anansi's wife.

Stop Think Write

PROBLEM AND SOLUTION

What is Anansi's problem? How does he attempt to deal with it?

_____

_____

_____

"Go back to work. I don't want to see you until suppertime."

As soon as the coast was clear, Anansi scurried back home. The kitchen was deserted, save for the bean stew bubbling in the pot.

"*Yum!*" Anansi cried. He grabbed a wooden spoon and started slurping hot soup. It was risky, but it was worth it.

After a few slurps, Anansi decided that spoonfuls were not enough. He pulled off his hat and filled it to the brim with steaming soup.

Just then his wife walked in.

Stop Think Write

UNDERSTANDING CHARACTERS

What details tell you that Anansi is greedy?

_____

_____

_____

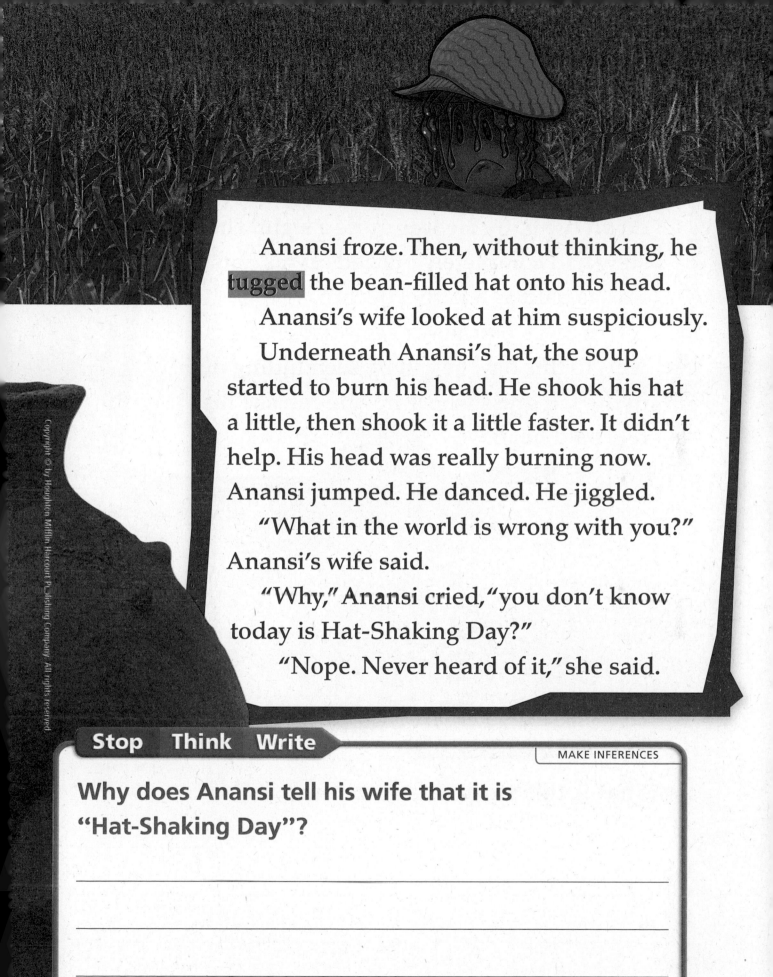

Anansi froze. Then, without thinking, he tugged the bean-filled hat onto his head.

Anansi's wife looked at him suspiciously.

Underneath Anansi's hat, the soup started to burn his head. He shook his hat a little, then shook it a little faster. It didn't help. His head was really burning now. Anansi jumped. He danced. He jiggled.

"What in the world is wrong with you?" Anansi's wife said.

"Why," Anansi cried, "you don't know today is Hat-Shaking Day?"

"Nope. Never heard of it," she said.

Stop | Think | Write

MAKE INFERENCES

Why does Anansi tell his wife that it is "Hat-Shaking Day"?

_____

_____

_____

119

When Anansi could stand it no longer, he ripped off his hat.

"*YEEEEEEEeeeeow!*"

Anansi went hooting and hollering down the path. He was quite a sight. The stew had completely burned off his hair. He was as bald as a kernel of corn.

Anansi's hair never grew back. That is why, to this day, he can be seen hiding out in the tall grass where no one can see his big, bald head.

Stop Think Write

THEME

What is this story meant to teach us?

_____

_____

_____

Look Back and Respond
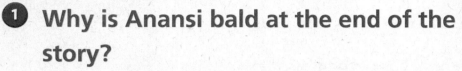

1 **Why is Anansi bald at the end of the story?**

Hint

For a clue, see page 120.

_____

_____

_____

2 **How are Anansi and his wife unlike each other?**

Hint

Think about their attitudes about work.

_____

_____

3 **Make up your own title for the story.**

Hint

Think about the story's lesson.

_____

_____

4 **How does the dialogue help you understand the characters?**

Hint

Think about what the dialogue reveals about the relationship between Anansi and his wife.

_____

_____

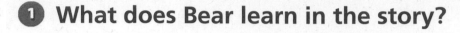

Be a Reading Detective!

Return to

"Tops and Bottoms"
Student Book pp. 431–453

1 **What does Bear learn in the story?**

☐ Hare is a great business partner.

☐ Corn is the most valuable crop.

☐ To succeed, a person must work hard.

Prove It! What evidence in the selection supports
your answer? Check the boxes. ☑ Make notes.

Evidence	Notes
☐ what Bear does while the Hares work	
☐ what happens to the crops Hare grows	
☐ how Bear changes at the end	

Write About It!

THEME

Answer question 1 using evidence from the text.

_____

_____

_____

_____

_____

_____

_____

2 **What traits help Hare do well in the end?**

☐ He is clever.

☐ He plans ahead.

☐ He is hardworking.

☐ other _____

Prove It! What evidence in the selection supports your answer? Check the boxes. ☑ Make notes.

Evidence	Notes
☐ what Hare says and does	
☐ the illustrations	
☐	

Write About It!

UNDERSTANDING CHARACTERS

Answer question 2 using evidence from the text.

_____

_____

_____

_____

_____

_____

_____

✓ **TARGET VOCABULARY**

fondly
mist
rugged
steep

Where the Iroquois Lived

1 Long ago, the Iroquois lived in what is now New York State. Much of the land had forests and steep hills.

Tell about a time when you climbed something <u>steep</u>.

_____

_____

_____

▲ **Trees on steep hills**

2 The ground in many places was rocky and rugged. It could be hard to walk on. The Iroquois traveled by canoe when they could.

Tell about a <u>rugged</u> area where you have been.

_____

_____

122

3 The Iroquois built longhouses and wigwams. Sometimes they awoke to find 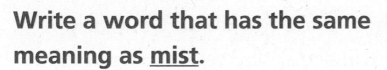 mist around their homes. The mist went away as the sun rose.

▲ **Mist in the trees**

Write a word that has the same meaning as <u>mist</u>.

_____

_____

_____

4 The Iroquois treated their children fondly. Adults rarely punished children or spoke harshly to them.

Tell about someone you treat <u>fondly</u>.

_____

_____

_____

Little Mud-Face

An American Indian Cinderella Tale
retold by Dina McClellan

Long ago, a hunter and his three daughters lived near a lake. Oldest Sister and Middle Sister were mean to their little sister. They made her do all the work.

The little sister had to cook and clean. She carried heavy sticks for the fire. Her face and arms were always dirty. People called her Little Mud-Face.

Stop   Think   Write

STORY STRUCTURE

Why is the little sister known as Little Mud-Face?

_____

_____

_____

124

Across the lake was the wigwam of
Strong Wind and his sister, Bright Eyes.
Bright Eyes loved her brother very much.
She could see and hear him. Most other
people could not.

One day, Bright Eyes came to the village.
"Strong Wind and I are looking for someone
to join our happy family," she said. "Only
someone who tells the truth may live with us."

Stop   Think   Write

COMPARE AND CONTRAST

**How is Bright Eyes different from most
other people?**

_____

_____

_____

125

Oldest Sister put on her best clothes. She found Bright Eyes by the lake.

"Strong Wind is out fishing," said Bright Eyes. "Can you see him in his canoe?"

"Of course I can," said Oldest Sister.

"What is his bowstring made of?" Bright Eyes asked.

"The hide of a deer," said Oldest Sister.

"Go home now," said Bright Eyes.

Why does Bright Eyes tell Oldest Sister to go home?

_____

_____

_____

The next day Middle Sister set off. She, too, found Bright Eyes by the lake.

"Do you see my brother near his canoe?"

"Of course," said Middle Sister.

"Then what is his bowstring made of?"

"Braided grass," said Middle Sister.

"Go home now," said Bright Eyes.

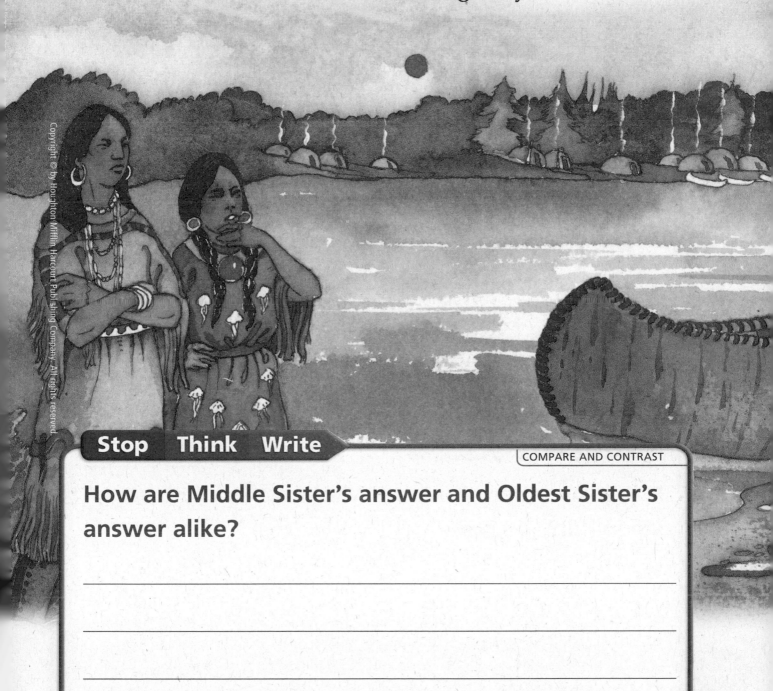

Stop Think Write

COMPARE AND CONTRAST

How are Middle Sister's answer and Oldest Sister's answer alike?

_____

_____

_____

127

The next day Little Mud-Face told her sisters that she would find Bright Eyes and Strong Wind. She would show them that she spoke the truth. Her sisters burst out laughing. Little Mud-Face didn't care.

She started walking around the lake. The land was rugged. Little Mud-Face climbed steep hills. She walked without pausing to catch her breath.

Stop   Think   Write

VOCABULARY

Is it easy or hard for Little Mud-Face to climb a <u>steep</u> hill?

_____

_____

_____

At last Little Mud-Face reached the lake. The water was covered with **mist**. Bright Eyes was waiting for her.

"Can you see my brother?" she asked.

"Oh, yes," said Little Mud-Face. "How special he is! He has a bowstring made from a rainbow!"

Stop Think Write

VOCABULARY

What does Little Mud-Face see through the mist?

_____

_____

_____

"You are right, Little Mud-Face," said Bright Eyes. "Only now you will be Rainbow Star." She led the girl to her wigwam. She cleaned her face and gave her a beautiful robe to wear.

Then Strong Wind came in. He looked at Rainbow Star fondly. "Someone who tells the truth will always be able to see the truth," he said. "From now on, you will be part of our family."

Stop   Think   Write

CONCLUSIONS

Why does Bright Eyes change Little Mud-Face's name to "Rainbow Star"?

_____

_____

_____

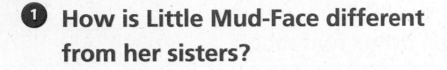
Look Back and Respond

1 How is Little Mud-Face different from her sisters?

Hint
Look on pages 126, 127, 129, and 130.

_____

_____

_____

2 How do you know that Little Mud-Face wants very much to show Bright Eyes and Strong Wind that she tells the truth?

Hint
Look on page 128.

_____

_____

_____

3 How is Strong Wind different from the other characters in the story?

Hint
Look on page 125.

_____

_____

_____

Be a Reading Detective!

Return to

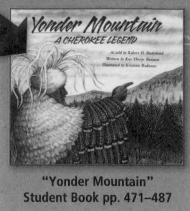

"Yonder Mountain"
Student Book pp. 471–487

1 What does Soaring Eagle do that is different from the other two men?

☐ He goes all the way to the top.

☐ He brings back a precious object.

☐ He is trying to be the new chief.

Prove It! What evidence in the selection supports your answer? Check the boxes. ☑ Make notes.

Evidence	Notes
☐ what Chief Sky says	
☐ what the men say	
☐ the illustrations	

Write About It!

COMPARE AND CONTRAST

Answer question **1** using evidence from the text.

_____

_____

_____

_____

_____

_____

_____

2 Does the old chief choose Soaring Eagle to be chief because he goes to the mountaintop?

☐ yes   ☐ no   ☐ no way to tell

Prove It! What evidence in the selection supports your answer? Check the boxes. ☑ Make notes.

Evidence	Notes
☐ the task Chief Sky gives the men	
☐ what the three men do and say	
☐ what Chief Sky says and does	
☐ the illustrations	

Write About It!

CONCLUSIONS

Answer question **2** using evidence from the text.

_____

_____

_____

_____

_____

_____

✓ **TARGET VOCABULARY**

ability

loyal

lying

partners

Smart Animals

Check the answer.

1 Dolphins have the _____ to talk to each other. They make special sounds that other dolphins understand.

☐ **principal**   ☐ **ability**   ☐ **customers**

2 Humpback whales work as _____ to get food. One whale blows bubbles under a group of fish. The other whale makes sounds to scare the fish. Fish swim to the surface, and whales eat them.

☐ **partners**   ☐ **fans**   ☐ **applause**

3 Dogs spend time _____ around when nobody is home. They know the usual times that people come home. Then they wait by the door or look out the window.

☐ **lying**   ☐ **pausing**   ☐ **tracing**

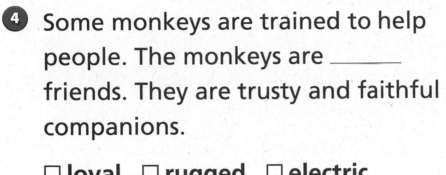

4 Some monkeys are trained to help people. The monkeys are _____ friends. They are trusty and faithful companions.

☐ **loyal**   ☐ **rugged**   ☐ **electric**

5 What special <u>ability</u> would you like to have? Why?

_____

_____

_____

6 Why is it good to have <u>partners</u> when there is a hard job to do?

_____

_____

_____

Dogs That Help

by Lois Grippo

Who doesn't love their dog? Dogs wait for us to come home. They sleep next to our beds. They bark when they hear strange footsteps. They're always around.

Being a friend is not the only thing a dog can do. For some people, a dog is an important helper. A dog can guide a person who can't see. It can nudge someone who can't hear. A dog can also bring things to a person who can't walk.

Stop · Think · Write

AUTHOR'S PURPOSE

How does the author feel about dogs?
How can you tell?

_____

_____

_____

Training

How does a puppy become a helper dog? It must go to school! These schools are special places. Dog trainers work at the schools. They teach dogs how to take care of people with special needs.

A helper dog has a lot to learn. It has to learn the difference between a red light and a green light. It has to learn how to act on a bus and with other animals. It must learn to obey its owner.

A helper dog at work

Stop   Think   Write

CAUSE AND EFFECT

Why must a dog go to school before it can become a helper dog?

_____

_____

_____

135

Getting Started

A helper dog must learn to do special jobs. What jobs must a dog learn? It depends on its owner's needs. Trainers make sure a dog can do the jobs that the person needs.

At last, a trained dog and its new owner meet. They learn how to live as partners. The dog helps its owner. The owner cares for the dog.

A helper dog and its owner are partners.

Stop Think Write

VOCABULARY

Why does the author say that the dog and its owner are <u>partners</u>?

_____

_____

_____

Seeing-Eye Dogs

Seeing-eye dogs are one kind of helper dog. Their job is to see for a person who cannot.

A seeing-eye dog helps its owner at home and outdoors. The dog leads its owner from place to place. It does not walk too fast or too slow. It protects its owner.

Seeing-eye dogs are smart. They stop when they see a red light. They lead their owner across a street when the light turns green.

Stop Think Write

MAIN IDEAS AND DETAILS

How do seeing-eye dogs help their owners?

_____

_____

_____

Hearing for an Owner

Sounds give information. Many give a warning. Babies cry. Horns honk. Alarms ring. Some people do not have the ability to hear. They won't know if there is trouble.

Some dogs are trained to hear for their owners. They are taught to listen for different sounds. The dog may be sleeping or lying down. When there is a noise, the dog jumps into action. It runs to its owner. It alerts him or her to the sound.

Stop   Think   Write

INFER AND PREDICT

If a person can't hear, how might a helper dog warn him or her that someone is at the door?

_____

_____

_____

Heroes

Some people are unable to walk. They can use a wheelchair. However, there are still some things they can't do.

Dogs can be trained to help these people. The dogs are taught to pick things up. They learn to turn lights on and off. They are even trained to push a wheelchair.

Helper dogs are heroes and loyal friends. They serve people with special needs. What do they ask for in return? Nothing more than a meal and a pat on the back!

Stop | Think | Write

VOCABULARY

What makes a helper dog a _loyal_ friend?

_____

_____

_____

Caring for a Dog

Dogs take care of people. People need to know how to take care of dogs.

- Dogs need to run. Be sure to take your dog outside at least two times each day.

- Dogs need to visit the doctor, just like people. They need special shots to help them stay healthy.

- Keep your dog clean. Brush its coat. Give your dog a bath.

- Feed your dog healthy food. Be sure to give your dog plenty of water, too.

- Be as loving and loyal to your dog as your dog is to you!

Stop   Think   Write

AUTHOR'S PURPOSE

Why does the author tell you how to care for a dog?

_____

_____

_____

1 Do you think the author wrote this story to persuade the reader to get a helper dog? Why or why not?

Hint

Clues you can use are on almost every page. For example, see pages 135 and 137.

_____

_____

_____

2 What are two things a helper dog might do for a person who can't walk?

Hint

For clues, see page 139.

_____

_____

_____

3 What are two ways that a person can take care of a dog?

Hint

For clues, see page 140.

_____

_____

_____

Be a Reading Detective!

Return to

"Aero and Officer Mike"
Student Book pp. 505–521

1 Why did the author write this selection?

☐ to tell about made-up characters

☐ to tell about real police dogs

☐ to tell which dogs make the best police dogs

Prove It! What evidence in the selection supports your answer? Check the boxes. ☑ Make notes.

Evidence	Notes
☐ facts about Aero's work	
☐ facts about police dog training	
☐ facts about a K-9's sense of smell	
☐ the photos	

Write About It!

AUTHOR'S PURPOSE

Answer question **1** using evidence from the text.

_____

_____

_____

_____

_____

_____

_____

EMERG
CALL 9-

141A

2 **What is the most important idea in the selection?**

☐ Aero and Officer Mike are partners.

☐ They ride in a special police car.

☐ Dogs can run much faster than people.

Prove It! What evidence in the selection supports your answer? Check the boxes. ☑ Make notes.

Evidence	Notes
☐ details about Aero's jobs	
☐ details about Aero's training	
☐ the photos	
☐	

POLICE

Write About It!

MAIN IDEAS AND DETAILS

Answer question 2 using evidence from the text.

_____

_____

_____

_____

_____

_____

anxiously
ingredients
remarked
tense

A Breakfast Surprise

It was Mom's birthday. Marta and Elena wanted to make breakfast for her. Marta and Elena looked anxiously at each other. What could they make?

Dad came into the kitchen. He saw that Marta and Elena looked tense. "Mom likes banana pancakes," he said. "First we'll get the ingredients."

Dad got eggs, milk, and flour. Marta and Elena mashed up bananas. They mixed everything in a bowl.

Dad cooked the pancakes. Marta and Elena took the pancakes to Mom. She hugged the girls. "This is the best birthday ever," she remarked.

1 You would feel good if someone _____ that you did something really well.

2 It is important to get the _____ you need before you start to cook.

3 Friends who are nervous about taking a test might look _____ at each other.

4 Write a word that means the opposite of <u>tense</u>.

_____

5 Write a word that has the same meaning as <u>remarked</u>.

_____

Swedish Meatball Potstickers with Mustard Dipping Sauce

by
Margaret Maugenest

Ava's class was having a food fair. Ava was on the planning team. She came home after the meeting. She threw her bag down. She slumped in a chair. She looked glum.

Stop Think Write

UNDERSTANDING CHARACTERS

How does Ava feel? How can you tell?

_____

_____

_____

"What's the matter?" her mom asked.

"I have to bring food for the fair," said Ava. "The food must tell about my family. I can only bring one dish."

"Make your Chinese potstickers. They're yummy!" Mom remarked.

"I don't want to. I make them all the time," said Ava.

Potstickers

Stop Think Write

VOCABULARY

How did Ava react when her mom **remarked** that Ava's potstickers are yummy?

_____

_____

_____

"What about Grandma Ida's Swedish meatballs? She made them in Sweden," said Mom. "She still makes them."

Ava shook her head. "I like the meatballs," she said. "I just don't want to make them for the food fair."

No dish sounded right. Ava looked at her mom **anxiously**. What could Ava bring?

Stop **Think** **Write**

How does Ava feel about her mom's ideas?

_____

_____

_____

"What about Dad's side of the family?" Mom said. "They came from Poland. You can make Polish food. Dad's mom was a great cook. I have her recipes."

Ava's mom got a folder. "Let's see. There is Polish stuffed cabbage. There is fish spread. There is mustard dipping sauce, too. These foods are easy to make. They are also very tasty!"

Stop   Think   Write

CONCLUSIONS

How can you tell that Ava's mom wants to be helpful?

_____

_____

_____

Ava was not listening. She stared at the floor. Her face had a big frown. She was tense and worried.

"What's the matter?" Mom asked.

"I can only bring one dish. I don't have a one-dish story! There is more than one part of me. There's the part that was born in China. Then there's the Swedish part, from you. There's also the Polish part from Dad!"

Stop   Think   Write

Why is Ava <u>tense</u> about bringing one dish?

_____

_____

_____

Mom gave Ava a big hug. "Don't worry. We will find the perfect dish to tell your story," she said.

"A combo dish?" asked Ava.

"Yes. Let's think of something new," said Mom.

Ava's eyes lit up. There was a big smile on her face.

Stop   Think   Write

UNDERSTANDING CHARACTERS

How does Ava feel now?

_____

_____

_____

"How about Polish stuffed cabbage? I can make it with Chinese soy sauce and Swedish jam," Ava said.

"I'm not sure about the jam," said Mom. "Could we do potstickers with fish spread?"

"Yech!" said Ava. Then she smiled. "I know! I'll make Swedish meatball potstickers with mustard dipping sauce."

"That sounds great!" said Mom. "Let's get the ingredients and start!"

Stop   Think   Write

Where might Ava and her mom get the ingredients they need?

_____

_____

_____

Look Back and Respond

1 Write two words that tell about Ava's mom.

_____

_____

Hint

Clues you can use are on almost every page!

2 What are the different parts of Ava's family background?

_____

_____

_____

Hint

For a clue, see page 148.

3 Why is Ava happy to make a combo dish?

_____

_____

_____

Hint

For a clue, see page 149.

Be a Reading Detective!

Return to

"The Extra-good Sunday"
Student Book pp. 539–557

1 Which word best describes Ramona?

☐ angry   ☐ hungry

☐ perfect   ☐ messy

Prove It! What evidence in the selection supports your answer? Check the boxes. ☑ Make notes.

Evidence	Notes
☐ what Ramona says and thinks	
☐ what happens in the story	
☐ the illustrations	

Write About It!

UNDERSTANDING CHARACTERS

Answer question **1** using evidence from the text.

_____

_____

_____

_____

_____

_____

_____

2 **Why do Beezus and Ramona have trouble making all the dishes? (Check all that are true.)**

☐ They don't have any recipes.

☐ They don't check the ingredients first.

☐ The dishes need different oven temperatures.

Prove It! What evidence in the selection supports your answer? Check the boxes. ☑ Make notes.

Evidence	Notes
☐ what Ramona says or does	
☐ what Beezus says or does	
☐ what the author tells us directly	
☐ the illustrations	

Write About It!

CAUSE AND EFFECT

Answer question 2 using evidence from the text.

_____

_____

_____

_____

_____

_____

_____

carton
project
recycle
rubbish

Recycling

Check the answer.

1 The United States makes a lot of
_____. We dump it in landfills.
We also burn it.

☐ **rubbish** ☐ **ingredients** ☐ **charts**

2 We can make less waste. We can
_____! We can reuse the materials.
We can use one thing to make
another.

☐ **imagine** ☐ **erupt** ☐ **recycle**

3 You can recycle many things.
Plastic bottles can become chairs.
A _____ can become paper.

☐ **harvest** ☐ **carton** ☐ **tide**

4 You can take things to a recycling center. You can reuse items at home. You can use cans or boxes for a school _____.

☐ **project**   ☐ **rubbish**   ☐ **advice**

5 Where would you put an empty milk <u>carton</u>?

_____

_____

_____

6 What kinds of things does your school <u>recycle</u>?

_____

_____

_____

Mark's Idea

by Dina McClellan

Jamal's class is learning about recycling. The kids have to do special work. They have to show how they recycle.

Jamal wants to make a video. He asks Jen, Paul, and Mark to help.

Jamal writes some notes. He talks them over with his teacher. She likes his ideas. The project is a go!

Stop Think Write

STORY STRUCTURE

What happens at the beginning of this story?

Jamal and his friends go to the teachers' room. Mr. Ruiz sees them.

"What's up?" asks Mr. Ruiz.

"We're making a video about recycling," says Paul. "Can we film the trash in the teachers' room?"

Mr. Ruiz smiles. "A video about recycling? That's a great idea!" he says. "Mrs. Hill is here, too. Maybe we can help."

Stop   Think   Write

AUTHOR'S PURPOSE

Mr. Ruiz says a video about recycling is a great idea. Would the author of this story agree? Explain.

_____

_____

_____

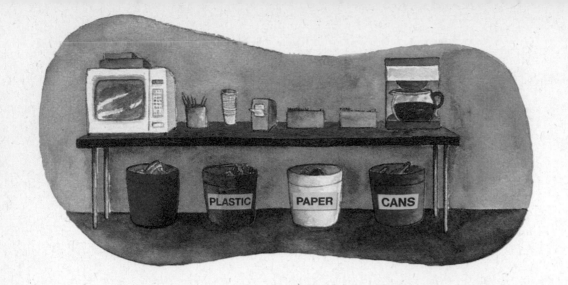

Jen has the camera. She zooms in on the rubbish. There are four trash bins. One is for plastic. One is for paper. One is for cans. One is for all other trash. Everything is in order.

Jen aims the camera at Mr. Ruiz and Mrs. Hill. They tell about how teachers recycle. When they are done, the kids thank the teachers. Then the kids leave.

"Our video has good facts. Still, I don't think it is much fun," Jamal says.

Stop Think Write

Why do the teachers put the <u>rubbish</u> in separate bins?

_____

_____

_____

"Let's see how students recycle," Jen says. "That might be fun."

The kids go to the student lunchroom. Jamal has the camera. Jen and Paul smile. "Here is a bin for cans," says Paul. "Inside we see—"

Paul stops. He frowns. "I see plastic bags, bottles, and a milk carton!" he says. "They don't belong in there!"

"Stop the camera!" says Jen.

Stop **Think** **Write**

CAUSE AND EFFECT

Why does Jen say, "Stop the camera!"?

_____

_____

_____

"The project is in trouble!" Jen says. "Kids are putting things in the wrong bins. We can't make a video about that!"

"I know what to do!" Mark says. "We don't have to just talk about recycling. We can make a how-to video. We can show how it's done!"

Stop   Think   Write

VOCABULARY

Why does Jen think the project is in trouble?

_____

_____

_____

158

Jen and Paul stand by the bins. Mark turns on the camera.

"Bags and cartons don't go with cans," Paul says. "We can show how to recycle the right way!"

Jen and Paul pick up some trash. They put it in the right bins.

Jamal smiles. "This is more fun," he says. "Our video will be great!"

Stop Think Write

STORY STRUCTURE

Explain how the story ending is like or different from what you expected.

_____

_____

_____

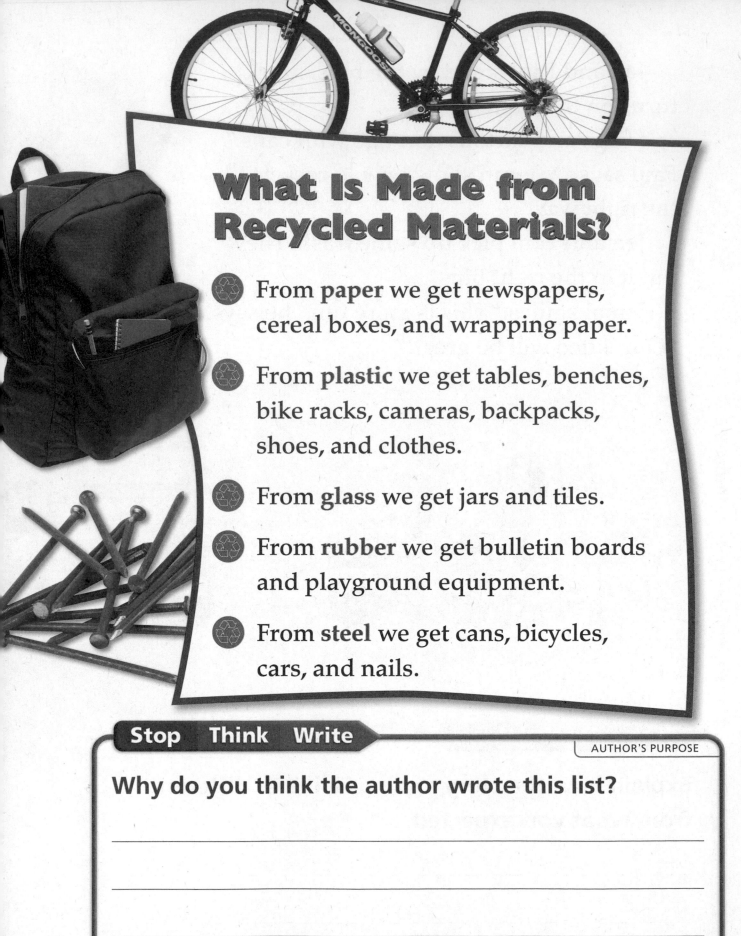

What Is Made from Recycled Materials?

From **paper** we get newspapers, cereal boxes, and wrapping paper.

From **plastic** we get tables, benches, bike racks, cameras, backpacks, shoes, and clothes.

From **glass** we get jars and tiles.

From **rubber** we get bulletin boards and playground equipment.

From **steel** we get cans, bicycles, cars, and nails.

Stop   Think   Write

AUTHOR'S PURPOSE

Why do you think the author wrote this list?

_____

_____

_____

Look Back and Respond

1 **What did you learn about recycling from this story?**

Hint

For clues, see pages 156, 157, and 160.

_____

_____

_____

2 **Why do the students end up making a how-to video?**

Hint

For clues, see pages 157 and 158.

_____

_____

_____

3 **Does the author think recycling is important? Explain why or why not.**

Hint

Your answer to questions 1 and 2 should help you.

_____

_____

_____

Be a Reading Detective!

1 **What story event makes Judy decide to start a compost bucket?**

☐ She watches a TV program.

☐ Her cat eats a banana.

☐ Mr. Todd tells the class to help the planet.

"Judy Moody Saves the World!"
Student Book pp. 15–37

Prove It! What evidence in the story supports your answer? Check the boxes. ☑ Make notes.

Evidence	Notes
☐ what Judy says and does	
☐ what other characters say and do	
☐ the illustrations	

Write About It!

STORY STRUCTURE

Answer question 1 using evidence from the text.

_____

_____

_____

_____

_____

_____

_____

2 **Does Judy think that Mr. Todd is a good teacher?**

☐ yes   ☐ no   ☐ no way to know

Prove It! What evidence in the story supports your answer? Check the boxes. ☑ Make notes.

Evidence	Notes
☐ what Judy says and does in class	
☐ what Mr. Todd says and does in class	
☐ what Judy does at home	

Write About It!

CONCLUSIONS

Answer question 2 using evidence from the text.

_____

_____

_____

_____

_____

_____

_____

✓ TARGET VOCABULARY

buried
evidence
fierce
fossils
remains

Studying Animals from the Past

1 Many animals from the past are not alive today. We can learn about them only from their remains.

What types of remains might an animal leave?

_____

_____

_____

2 Experts dig to find the bones of these animals. The bones are buried under dirt and rock.

Why must people be careful when digging up buried animal bones?

_____

_____

_____

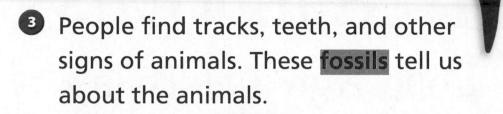

3 People find tracks, teeth, and other signs of animals. These <mark>fossils</mark> tell us about the animals.

What <u>fossils</u> would you like to see?

_____

_____

_____

4 Bones and tracks are not the only <mark>evidence</mark> we have. Cave paintings also tell us about animals from the past.

When you visit a friend's house, what <u>evidence</u> tells you that there is a pet?

_____

_____

_____

5 Some cave paintings show <mark>fierce</mark> beasts. They may be fighting.

Name one <u>fierce</u> animal alive today.

_____

Mammoths
Long Ago and Today

by Candyce Norvell

Our world is full of big animals. Still, no beast on land today is as big as a mammoth. Mammoths lived in the past.

Many mammoths lived during the Ice Age. Much of the land on Earth was frozen. Mammoths had to be tough to stand the cold. They had thick coats of hair. They had body fat to keep them warm. A mammoth weighed about 6,000 pounds.

Stop   Think   Write

MAIN IDEAS AND DETAILS

Write two details that show that mammoths were large, tough animals.

_____

_____

_____

Plant Eaters

Mammoths did not hunt other animals. They were plant eaters. They used their trunks to get tree leaves. They pulled plants from the ground, too. They used large, flat teeth to grind up the plants.

A mammoth's trunk had other uses, too. It gave mammoths a great sense of smell. It let them move rocks and trees out of the way. Mammoths may have locked trunks to say hello.

Stop Think Write

MAIN IDEAS AND DETAILS

How did mammoths use their trunks?

_____

_____

_____

Life in a Mammoth Pack

Mammoths lived together in packs. A pack had several families. Each pack had a leader. The leader was the oldest or strongest mother mammoth.

Mammoths in a pack did not always get along. They could be fierce. Sometimes they fought with their tusks. The tusks were about ten feet long. They were tough weapons. The tusks could also dig through snow to get plants.

Stop Think Write

CONCLUSIONS AND GENERALIZATIONS

Why do you think mammoths roamed in packs?

_____

_____

_____

Mammoths and People

People hunted mammoths. Hunters fought the beasts with stone weapons. They ate the meat. They used the bones to make weapons and tools.

Experts think that hunters prized mammoths. Hunters made paintings of mammoths in caves. The paintings show mammoths as they really looked. This is **evidence** that hunters knew the animals well.

Stop · Think · Write

VOCABULARY

What <u>evidence</u> is there that people knew mammoths well?

_____

_____

_____

A Mammoth Find

Mammoths died out long ago. Even so, we know how big they were. In 1974, a large number of bones were found. They were found in a hill in Hot Springs, South Dakota. Workers wanted to put houses on the hill. They brought in big trucks. When they dug, they found giant bones! They were the bones of mammoths. Experts learned a lot from the bones.

◄ 1

2 ▼

Stop   Think   Write

CONCLUSIONS AND GENERALIZATIONS

How did people find out how big mammoths were?

_____

_____

_____

3 ▶

4 ▶

Long ago, this land was a deep hole. The hole was full of water and sticky clay. Maybe the animals tried to get a drink and got stuck. They tried to get out, but they could not.

Over time, the spring ran dry. The animal **remains** were **buried**. Their bones were not found for thousands of years. Now Hot Springs is one of the best places to learn about mammoths.

Stop **Think** **Write**

VOCABULARY

What kind of mammoth <u>remains</u> were found in Hot Springs?

_____

_____

_____

Mammoths in Our World Today

The last mammoth died thousands of years ago. How and why did this happen?

Experts think it got too warm too fast. Plants began to die. Then mammoths didn't have food. Perhaps hunters wiped out the mammoths. We may never know.

We study fossils to learn about mammoths. Their story can help us protect animals that live today.

Stop   Think   Write

Why doesn't the author tell us why no mammoths are alive today?

_____

_____

_____

Look Back and Respond

1 Why is Hot Springs a good place to learn about mammoths?

Hint

For clues, see pages 168 and 169.

_____

_____

_____

2 What did mammoths eat? How do you think we know that?

Hint

For a clue, see page 165.

_____

_____

_____

3 The author gives two reasons why the mammoths might have died out. Which reason seems more likely to you? Why?

Hint

For clues, see page 170.

_____

_____

_____

Be a Reading Detective!

1 How were scientists able to conclude that albertosaurs were meat-eaters?

"The Albertosaurus Mystery"
Student Book pp. 59–75

☐ from their fossil eggs

☐ from their teeth and jaws

☐ from how they were buried

Prove It! What evidence in the selection supports your answer? Check the boxes. ☑ Make notes.

Evidence	Notes
☐ what the text says	
☐ what the captions say	
☐ the photos and drawings	

Write About It!

CONCLUSIONS

Answer question **1** using evidence from the text.

_____

_____

_____

_____

_____

_____

2 What caused Philip Currie to go looking in the badlands for albertosaurs?

☐ a map made by Barnum Brown

☐ albertosaur bones in the museum

☐ a phone call from Rodolfo Coria

Prove It! What evidence in the selection supports your answer? Check the boxes. ☑ Make notes.

Evidence	Notes
☐ what Barnum Brown did	
☐ what Philip Currie did	
☐ clues from the titles and captions	
☐ photos and other illustrations	

Write About It!

CAUSE AND EFFECT

Answer question **2** using evidence from the text.

_____

_____

_____

_____

_____

_____

Trees

Trees do more than give shade. A tree makes its own food. The leaves make food. They use energy from the sun. Trees have tubes inside them. They carry food to the roots. Roots can store food.

Tree leaves come in many shapes and sizes. Some leaves are soft. Other leaves have waxy coverings. Some leaves grow in clumps. They bunch together.

Trees need water to live and grow. The roots absorb water. Water moves throughout the tree in its tubes.

1. Some leaves grow in _____, or groups.

2. The _____ of some leaves are waxy.

3. Water travels _____ the tree in its tubes.

4. What is another way to say <u>absorb</u>?

_____

5. What do you <u>store</u> in your room?

_____

_____

_____

The Life of a Hickory Tree

by Dina McClellan

It is fall in the forest. Squirrels are busy. They are looking for nuts. They need to store the nuts. They save them to eat in the winter.

This squirrel does not save all the nuts. He eats one now. He cracks the shell. Then he eats the tasty nut.

Stop   Think   Write

TEXT AND GRAPHIC FEATURES

Which part of the text best matches what is happening in the picture?

_____

_____

_____

174

A Lucky Nut

Another squirrel finds a hickory nut. He hears a noise. He drops the nut and runs away.

The nut hits a stone. It bounces to the ground. Soon, leaves fall on the nut. They hide it.

This is a lucky nut. It will grow into a hickory tree. Most other nuts will not. Squirrels and other animals will eat them.

Stop   Think   Write

TEXT AND GRAPHIC FEATURES

Does the heading "A Lucky Nut" tell about the text on this page? How?

_____

_____

_____

Hidden from Sight

Even bears like to eat hickory nuts. They eat them whenever they can.

Bears do not find this hidden nut. The shell of the nut rots. During winter, the nut sinks into the soil.

Animals are looking for food in the forest. Rabbits and mice do not find the nut. It is buried deep in the ground.

Stop | **Think** | **Write**

CAUSE AND EFFECT

Why can't the animals find the nut?

_____

_____

_____

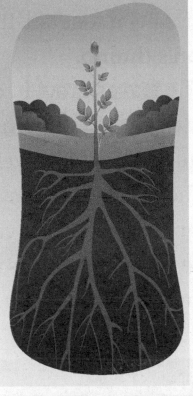

The Seed Sprouts

It is spring in the forest. The seed inside the nut sprouts. It grows roots. They go deep into the ground. The roots absorb water from the soil.

The little tree grows. Years pass. The big hickory tree makes more nuts. Most of them never sprout.

Stop   Think   Write

MAIN IDEAS AND DETAILS

Why are the roots of a tree so important?

_____

_____

_____

177

A Growing Tree

Time passes. After ten years, the tree is seven feet tall. It is as thick as a man's thumb.

The leaves grow in clumps of five. They are light green in the summer. In the fall, they turn yellow.

The tree faces many dangers. It can be chopped down. Fires can hurt it. Bugs may make holes in it. Birds may peck the holes and make them bigger.

Stop	Think	Write

VOCABULARY

Look at the <u>clumps</u> of leaves on the tree. How many leaves are in each clump?

_____

_____

_____

Getting Older

More time passes. After twenty years, the bark is still smooth. Now the tree is thirty years old. Its **coverings** start to split. Each part of the bark is tight in the middle. The edges curve away from the trunk. This makes the tree look shaggy.

After forty years, the first nuts appear. Some of the nuts take root. They might grow into trees. Hickory trees can live for 300 years!

Stop | **Think** | **Write**

TEXT AND GRAPHIC FEATURES

About how old is the tree in this picture? Look at the bark. Use the text to help you.

_____

_____

_____

The Cycle Goes On

It's fall in the forest. A squirrel comes out. It knows when the hickory tree has nuts. The squirrel looks for them.

Other animals look for nuts, too. Will they find all of the nuts? Will one lucky nut sprout in the spring?

Throughout the forest, trees are growing. Each one is in a different stage of life.

Stop   Think   Write

VOCABULARY

The picture shows other things that are happening throughout the forest at this time of year. Name three things you see.

_____

_____

_____

Look Back and Respond

1 **Which kinds of animals look for hickory nuts?**

Hint

For clues, see the sections called "A Lucky Nut" and "Hidden from Sight."

_____

_____

_____

2 **How does the hickory tree get water from the soil?**

Hint

For clues, see the section that has a heading about sprouting.

_____

_____

_____

3 **Look at the trees on the first and last pages of the story. Why do they look similar?**

Hint

Think about the story. Read the headings to remind yourself about the tree's life.

_____

_____

_____

Return to

"A Tree Is Growing"
Student Book pp. 93–115

Be a Reading Detective!

1 What facts does the selection give about oak trees?

☐ The leaves change color.

☐ Oak trees do not have flowers.

☐ Acorns are an oak's seeds.

Prove It! What evidence in the selection supports your answer? Check the boxes. ☑ Make notes.

Evidence	Notes
☐ the text	
☐ sidebars and captions	
☐ illustrations and labels	

Write About It!

TEXT AND GRAPHIC FEATURES

Answer question **1** using evidence from the text.

_____

_____

_____

_____

_____

_____

_____

2 **Which sentences below are main ideas that are supported by details in the selection?**

☐ Moles live under the ground.

☐ Trees grow and change throughout their lives.

☐ A tree's parts help it get food and stay safe.

Prove It! What evidence in the selection supports your answer? Check the boxes. ☑ Make notes.

Evidence	Notes
☐ details about moles	
☐ details about how trees grow	
☐ details about roots and bark	

Write About It!

MAIN IDEAS AND DETAILS

Answer question 2 using evidence from the text.

_____

_____

_____

_____

_____

_____

TARGET VOCABULARY

burden
drowsy
greedily
hesitation
ignores

Animals Are Not Allowed

"It's not fair!" said the old tree.

"Animals get ❶ _____

and fall asleep in our shade, they eat

❷ _____ from our

branches, and instead of being grateful

they leave a mess! And it stinks! Pee-ew!"

"I know!" said the young tree. "Let's

drive away any animal that comes by!"

"Bad idea," said the old tree. "The animals are a ③ _____,

but they serve a purpose. We all depend on each other—trees, animals, people. A young tree that

④ _____ his elders is a fool."

The young tree wouldn't listen. He drove away all the animals that very day. Soon after, people came to the forest to cut wood for their fire.

The wise old tree said, "Now men will come, without ⑤ _____. They have no fear without the animals."

The Enchanted Flute

from a Native
American Legend

adapted by Dina McClellan

Once there was a widow who had a son. They lived a simple life. In the evenings they would sit and look at the mountains far away.

As the son grew older, he felt the need to roam. He wondered what life was like on the other side of the mountains.

But the boy's mother warned him: *Never go across the mountains.*

And the boy never did.

Stop Think Write

CAUSE AND EFFECT

Why doesn't the boy ever go across the mountains?

_____

_____

_____

Still, the boy was curious. He loved his mother and his home, but it was time to see the world.

His mother understood.

"A mother who ignores her son's need to see the world is not a good mother," she said. "I will not be a burden to you."

To keep her son from harm, she gave him a flute. "This is not just any flute; it is magic. Play it if you need help."

The boy promised he would. Then he left.

Stop Think Write

STORY STRUCTURE

What is the boy planning to do?

_____

_____

_____

After days of traveling, the boy finally reached the place over the mountains.

It was another world! A world of lush, green pastures, sparkling lakes, and fast-flowing rivers. And animals! They flew and crawled and scampered and burrowed and slithered. It was a wonder!

This is where he wanted to be. He knew he would never be happy anywhere else.

Stop   Think   Write

MAIN IDEA AND DETAILS

How is the place over the mountains different from the boy's childhood home? What details tell you?

_____

_____

_____

As the boy continued walking, he found himself near a sparkling lake. He realized he was very hungry and had no food left. He would starve!

His mother's words came back to him. He took out the flute and played.

Suddenly the lake split open, and thousands of silvery fish burst out. The boy ate greedily. Afterward, he felt drowsy and lay down for a nap.

Little did the boy know that Rabbit had been hiding in the tall grass, spying on him.

Stop   Think   Write

STORY STRUCTURE

What new character has entered the scene? What do you think he is up to?

_____

_____

_____

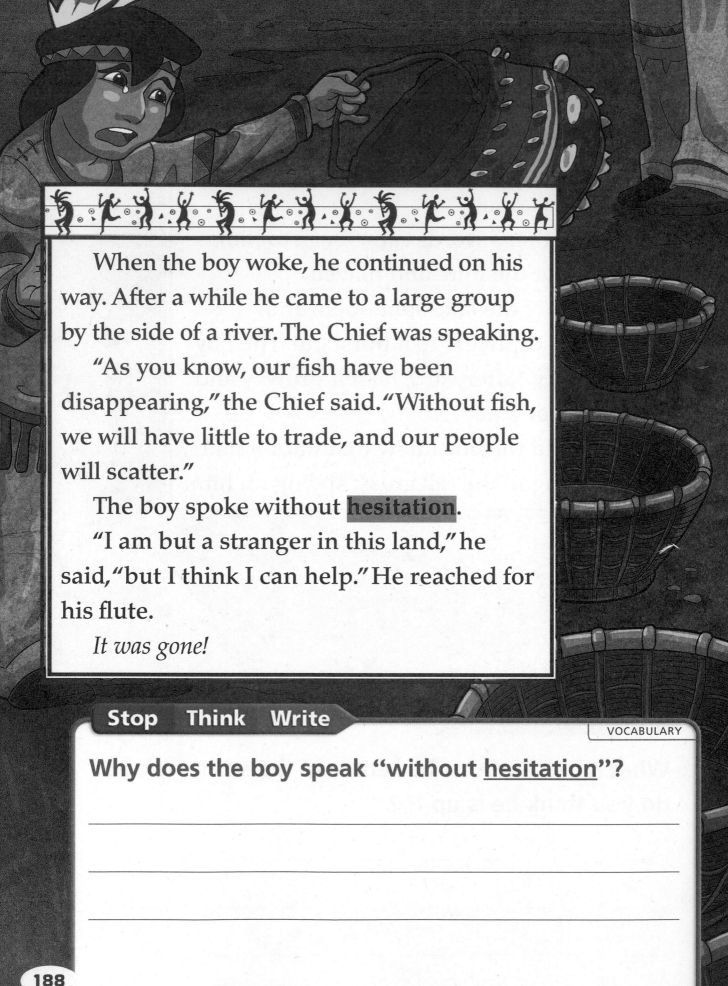

When the boy woke, he continued on his way. After a while he came to a large group by the side of a river. The Chief was speaking.

"As you know, our fish have been disappearing," the Chief said. "Without fish, we will have little to trade, and our people will scatter."

The boy spoke without hesitation.

"I am but a stranger in this land," he said, "but I think I can help." He reached for his flute.

It was gone!

Stop Think Write

Why does the boy speak "without <u>hesitation</u>"?

_____

_____

_____

"Don't listen to him!" screeched Rabbit. "He's no good! Only *I*, Rabbit, can help you!"

He held up the flute and waved it.

Then he blew into it. "*Ffffth . . . ftfff . . . Ffff!*" Nothing happened.

He tried again, more loudly this time. "*Ffffth . . . ftfff . . .*"

In an instant, Rabbit was surrounded by a thousand angry insects.

Stop   Think   Write

UNDERSTANDING CHARACTERS

What kind of character is Rabbit? Write a few words to describe him.

_____

_____

_____

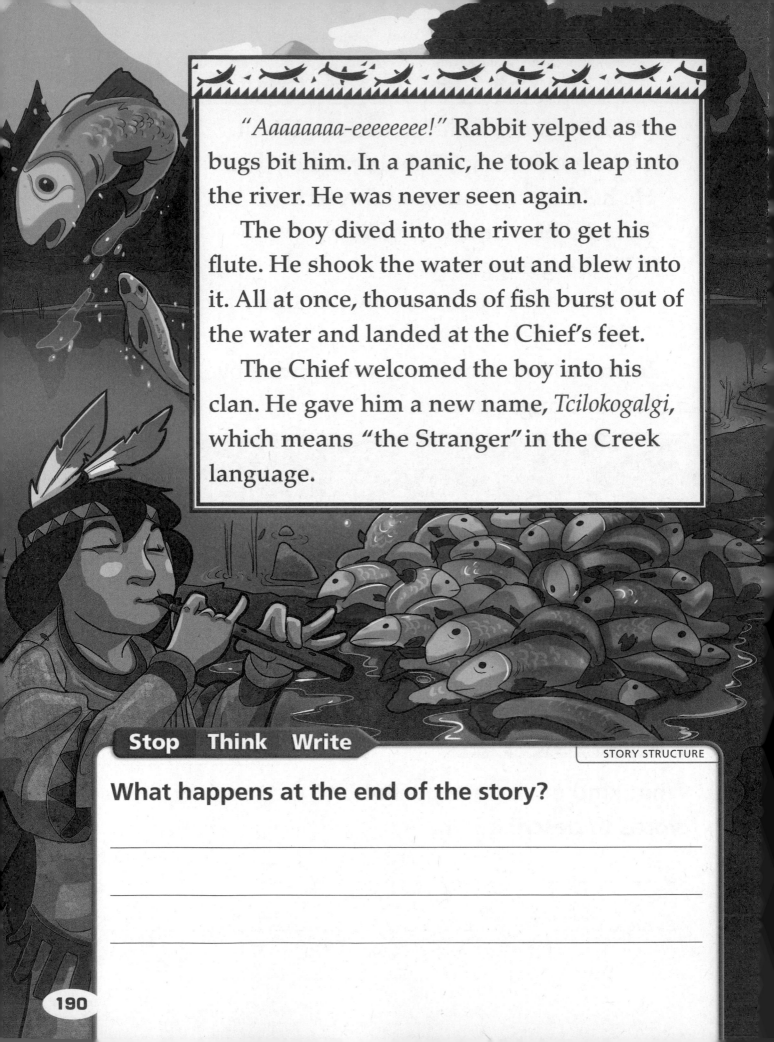

"*Aaaaaaaa-eeeeeeee!*" Rabbit yelped as the bugs bit him. In a panic, he took a leap into the river. He was never seen again.

The boy dived into the river to get his flute. He shook the water out and blew into it. All at once, thousands of fish burst out of the water and landed at the Chief's feet.

The Chief welcomed the boy into his clan. He gave him a new name, *Tcilokogalgi*, which means "the Stranger" in the Creek language.

Stop Think Write

STORY STRUCTURE

What happens at the end of the story?

_____

_____

_____

Look Back and Respond

1 Why does the boy's mother let him go across the mountains?

Hint

For a clue, see page 184.

_____

_____

_____

2 Why does the boy's flute disappear?

Hint

For a clue, see page 187.

_____

_____

_____

3 Why is Rabbit "never seen again"?

Hint

Think about the way Rabbit acts in the story.

_____

_____

_____

Be a Reading Detective!

Return to

"Two Bear Cubs"
Student Book pp. 133–151

1 **What important events happen in Scene 1?**

☐ Mother Grizzly looks for the cubs.

☐ A stone grows into a mountain.

☐ The cubs disobey their mother.

Prove It! What evidence in the play supports your answer? Check the boxes. ☑ Make notes.

Evidence	Notes
☐ scene headings	
☐ words spoken by the animals	
☐ words spoken by the Storyteller	

Write About It!

STORY STRUCTURE

Answer question 1 using evidence from the text.

_____

_____

_____

_____

_____

_____

191A _____

2 **In what way is Scene 2 different from Scene 3?**

☐ In Scene 2, no one knows where the bear cubs are.

☐ In Scene 3, one animal is able to climb to the cubs.

☐ In Scene 3, the mountain is no longer high.

Prove It! What evidence in the play supports your answer? Check the boxes. ☑ Make notes.

Evidence	Notes
☐ words spoken by the animals	
☐ words spoken by the Storyteller	
☐ illustrations	
☐ scene headings	

Write About It!

COMPARE AND CONTRAST

Answer question 2 using evidence from the text.

_____

_____

_____

_____

_____

_____

_____

✔ **TARGET VOCABULARY**

climate
constant
region
shelter
wilderness

Greenland

1 Greenland is the largest island in the world. The largest region of that island is covered in ice. The ice can be up to four feet deep.

What region of the world would you like to visit? Why?

_____

_____

_____

2 The climate of Greenland varies. In the north, the temperature is almost always below freezing.

Describe the climate where you live.

_____

_____

_____

3 During the summer, there is **constant** daylight.

Write a synonym for <u>constant</u>.

_____

4 Greenland is not all icy **wilderness**. Nuuk, the capital city, is like many big cities. It has buildings, traffic jams, and lots of people.

Why might people try to keep a <u>wilderness</u> area the way it is?

_____

_____

_____

5 Modern-day igloos called space huts give **shelter** in the coldest areas.

Name two kinds of <u>shelter</u> in your town.

_____

_____

A World of Ice

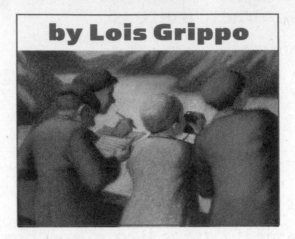

by Lois Grippo

Winter at Sea

It was the winter of 1933. Louise Arner Boyd had been at sea for six weeks. Louise was an explorer. She and her team were making a map. It was of the shore of northeast Greenland. The work was dangerous.

The land was an icy **wilderness**. There was no sign of life.

Stop **Think** **Write**

MAIN IDEAS AND DETAILS

What details tell you that the ship is in a cold place?

_____

_____

_____

The ship moved toward a glacier. Louise stared at the mountain of ice. She took photos. She made notes of everything she saw.

It was very cold. There was no shelter from the wind. Louise did not mind. "There is never any hardship in doing what interests you," she said.

Stop   Think   Write

VOCABULARY

What is the effect of having no <u>shelter</u> from the wind? Explain.

_____

_____

_____

Stuck!

All at once, the ship shook. Louise fell to her knees. There was a loud groan. The ship had run aground.

The captain said, "Reverse the engines!" The crew ran the engines at full speed. The ship didn't move.

They were stuck.

Stop   Think   Write

CAUSE AND EFFECT

Why did the ship suddenly shake?

_____

_____

_____

Northeast Greenland was a bad place to be stuck. The climate was harsh. In winter, it was the worst. Many cold and hungry explorers had died in this region.

There were no other ships nearby. There were no towns or villages. There was no one to save them. Louise and her team would have to save themselves.

Stop   Think   Write

VOCABULARY

Why is northeast Greenland a dangerous region in the winter?

_____

_____

_____

A Dangerous Situation

The tide was getting lower. The water level went down. The crew watched. Their **constant** worry was that the ship would tip over. If it did, they could do nothing.

The ship did not tip over.

When the tide came back in, the ship didn't float off the mud. It was too heavy. It was still stuck.

Stop | Think | Write

INFER AND PREDICT

Why would it be terrible if the ship tipped over?

_____

_____

_____

Louise Has a Plan

The crew had to make the ship lighter. The men took three boats off the ship. They unloaded oil and gas. They threw coal overboard.

The tide came in. The ship was still stuck. Louise saw a big iceberg. She had an idea. The crew tied a cable around the iceberg. They would try to pull themselves out of the mud!

Stop **Think** **Write**

MAIN IDEAS AND DETAILS

What did the crew do to make the ship lighter?

_____

_____

_____

The captain ordered the crew to start the engines. The cable was attached to a crank. The engines roared. The crank pulled the cable.

The cable stretched tightly. It began to pull the ship toward the iceberg. The ship lifted off the mud! It was floating again.

Louise's plan had worked. The ship moved safely out to sea.

Stop   Think   Write

CAUSE AND EFFECT

How did the crew get the ship out of the mud?

_____

_____

_____

Look Back and Respond

1 **What happened first, next, and last?**

Hint

You'll need to thumb through the whole story.

_____

_____

_____

2 **Why did the crew worry about the tide going down after the ship got stuck?**

Hint

For a clue, see page 198.

_____

_____

_____

3 **Would you like to explore a region like northeast Greenland? Explain.**

Hint

Details about the region are on pages 194, 195, and 197.

_____

_____

_____

Be a Reading Detective!

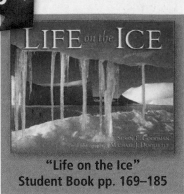

"Life on the Ice"
Student Book pp. 169–185

1 **Is it hard to live in a very cold place?**

☐ yes

☐ no

Prove It! What evidence in the selection supports your answer? Check the boxes. Make notes.

Evidence	Notes
☐ details about the clothes people wear at the Poles	
☐ details about the food people must eat	
☐ details about building shelters	
☐ the photos	

Write About It!

MAIN IDEAS AND DETAILS

Answer question 1 using evidence from the text.

_____

_____

_____

_____

_____

_____

_____

2 What are some reasons that scientists can use the ice at the North Pole to study air pollution?

☐ The ice is very old.

☐ The ice moves slowly toward the ocean.

☐ The ice has trapped air pollution.

Prove It! What evidence in the selection supports your answer? Check the boxes. ☑ Make notes.

Evidence	Notes
☐ details about the ice	
☐ details about what scientists do	
☐ the photos	

Write About It!

CAUSE AND EFFECT

Answer question **2** using evidence from the text.

_____

_____

_____

_____

_____

_____

_____

201B

batted
fetch
prairie
sniff
thumped

Pioneer Doctor

Life was hard for a doctor on the **prairie**. Often, a knock on the door would come in the middle of the night. The doctor would **fetch** his bag, saddle up his horse, and ride off. In the summer, he **batted** away mosquitoes as he rode. In the winter, he **thumped** across the frozen plain on snowshoes.

There were forest fires, floods, falls from horses, and hunting accidents.

The pioneer doctor tended to all these and more, armed only with his bag of medicines. There were herbs to eat, ointments to rub on, medicines to **sniff**—even a pair of "twisters" for pulling teeth.

For his services, the pioneer doctor was often paid in eggs, butter, hens, or apples. No wonder so many pioneer doctors left after a year or two. They went to seek another job back east!

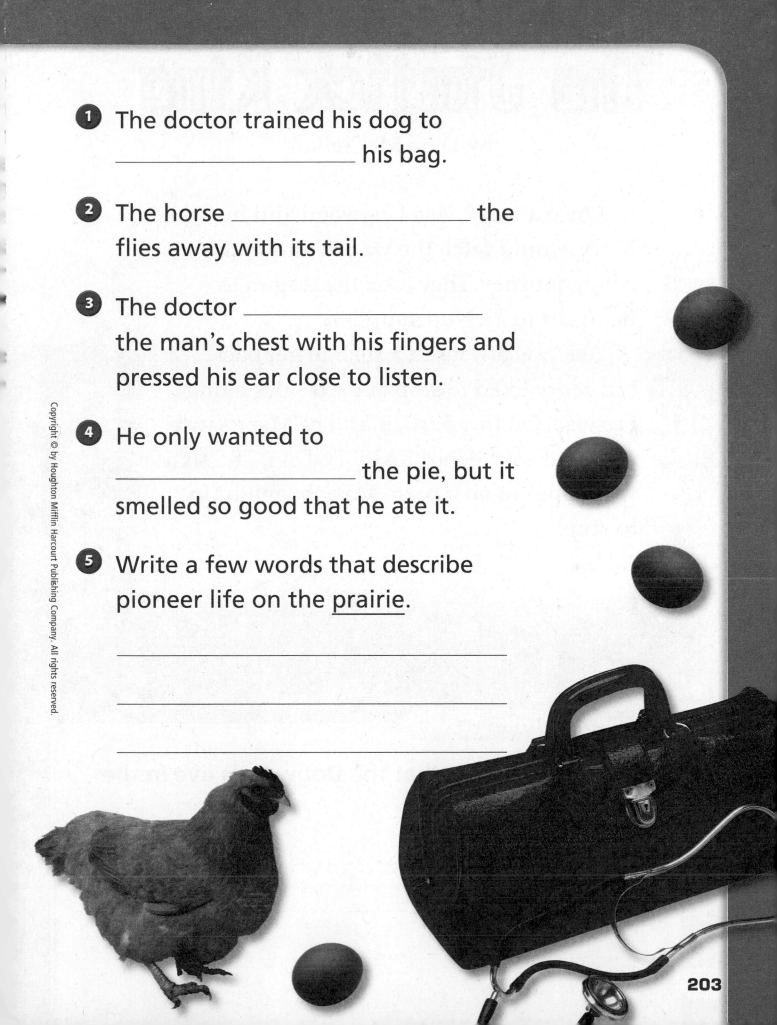

1 The doctor trained his dog to
_____ his bag.

2 The horse _____ the
flies away with its tail.

3 The doctor _____
the man's chest with his fingers and
pressed his ear close to listen.

4 He only wanted to
_____ the pie, but it
smelled so good that he ate it.

5 Write a few words that describe
pioneer life on the <u>prairie</u>.

_____

_____

_____

The Jimjick King

by Dina McClellan

Once a week, Asa Dogwood and his wife, Mary, would **fetch** the wagon and make a long journey. They took the wagon to Bearport to pick up supplies.

Asa was always in a rush to get back, but Mary liked to stop at barn sales along the way. On this particular day, Mary saw a sign that said JUNK SALE TODAY. The sign was hanging on a barn. Mary begged Asa to stop.

Stop   Think   Write

MAKE INFERENCES

What clues tell you that the Dogwoods live in the country?

_____

_____

_____

"Now, Mary," said Asa, sighing, "you know what's in there—the same silly things we have in *our* barn. We're always trying to get rid of the stuff!"

"Please, Asa?" Mary said. She smiled sweetly.

Of course, Asa agreed.

Together, they walked up to the farmhouse and knocked on the front door. A pleasant woman greeted them and led them to the barn.

Stop Think Write

Where do Asa and Mary stop on their way home from Bearport?

_____

_____

_____

Mary picked her way through piles of old furniture, clothing, rusted farm equipment, and bad family portraits. Asa wandered off, bored.

Then Asa's eyes landed on an object he couldn't identify. He picked it up. He turned it around. He thumped it on the table. He gave it a sniff. He decided to ask the pleasant woman what it was.

"It's a—a—a jimjick!" she said.

She doesn't know, Asa thought.

He bought it for twenty-five cents.

Stop Think Write

MAKE INFERENCES

Why does the woman say that the object is a "jimjick"?

_____

_____

_____

_____

When they got home, Asa showed Mary his new purchase.

"Ooooooooh! It's beautiful!" Mary exclaimed. "Um—what exactly is it?"

"It's called a jimjick," he said.

She furrowed her brow. "I've never heard of a jimjick."

"Oh, they're extremely rare," said her husband. "They can only be found here in Indiana."

Stop Think Write

STORY STRUCTURE

How does Asa try to fool Mary in this scene?

_____

_____

_____

The next time they drove into town, Mary suggested stopping at another barn sale. This time, Asa had no problem agreeing.

Another pleasant woman led them to a barn. Mary bought a painting of a prairie that looked like the view from their bedroom window. Asa bought an object very much like the first one. He batted off a cobweb and held it up.

"Another jimjick!" Mary clapped her hands in excitement.

Stop **Think** **Write**

MAKE INFERENCES

Why is Asa willing to stop at the barn sale?

_____

_____

_____

Asa built a fancy cabinet to show off his jimjicks. Word got around. Soon Asa was known as a collector of jimjicks.

Farmers all over the county were now on the lookout for jimjicks to buy. Soon it was hard to find any. Jimjick prices went up and up to 50 dollars each!

Whenever Asa found a jimjick, he bought it. He built a much bigger cabinet to show off his new jimjicks. He now had hundreds of them.

Stop **Think** **Write**

CAUSE AND EFFECT

Why do jimjicks go up in price?

_____

_____

_____

Asa was recognized as the country's leading expert on jimjicks. Many newspapers printed articles about him.

Soon Asa's cabinets could no longer hold all his jimjicks. He added a special room onto his house to show off the jimjicks. After Asa died, Mary turned this room into a museum.

Unfortunately, tragedy struck. About a hundred years ago, the Jimjick Museum was hit by lightning. It went up in flames, and all the jimjicks were destroyed. Since then, jimjicks have all but disappeared.

That's why you never see any.

Stop Think Write

According to the story, why do people today never see jimjicks at yard sales?

_____

_____

_____

Look Back and Respond

1 **What clues tell you where this story is set?**

Hint

There are clues on almost every page!

_____

_____

_____

2 **How does Asa become a jimjick expert?**

Hint

For clues, see pages 209 and 210.

_____

_____

_____

3 **What eventually happens to Asa's collection of jimjicks?**

Hint

For a clue, see page 210.

_____

_____

_____

Be a Reading Detective!

Return to

Sarah, Plain and Tall

"Sarah, Plain and Tall"
Student Book pp. 207–221

1 **How does Caleb feel about Sarah?**

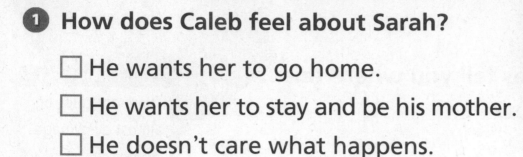

☐ He wants her to go home.

☐ He wants her to stay and be his mother.

☐ He doesn't care what happens.

Prove It! What evidence in the story supports your answer? Check the boxes. ☑ Make notes.

Evidence	Notes
☐ what Caleb says before Sarah arrives	
☐ what he says while picking flowers	
☐ how he acts at dinner	
☐	

Write About It!

STORY STRUCTURE

Answer question 1 using evidence from the text.

_____

_____

_____

_____

_____

_____

2 **Will Sarah stay with the Witting family?**

☐ yes   ☐ no   ☐ no way to know

Prove It! What evidence in the story supports
your answer? Check the boxes. ☑   Make notes.

Evidence	Notes
☐ what Sarah does with the flowers	
☐ what Sarah says about the hair	
☐ what Sarah sings	
☐	

Write About It!

CONCLUSIONS

Answer question ② using evidence from the text.

_____

_____

_____

_____

_____

_____

_____

✓ TARGET VOCABULARY

chilly
landscape
migrate
plenty
survival

Birds in Summer and Winter

1 All animals need food to live. They also need water for their survival.

Why is survival easier in spring and summer?

_____

_____

_____

2 There is plenty of food in spring and summer. There is not as much food in winter.

Do you have plenty of space in your backpack for all your books?

_____

_____

_____

3 The weather gets cold in winter. Many birds **migrate**. They go to warmer places.

What word has almost the same meaning as migrate?

_____

4 Ducks, geese, and swans fly south. You can see flocks of birds. They fly over the **landscape**.

Think of where you live. What things can you see in the landscape?

_____

_____

_____

5 In the spring, the weather gets warm. It is not so **chilly**. The birds come back.

What is the opposite of chilly?

_____

Snow Petrels

by Margaret Maugenest

Winter in Antarctica

Antarctica is a chilly place at the South Pole. It is the coldest place on Earth. Ice covers the ground all year.

Winter in Antarctica begins in June. The days are very short. There is no light in the sky. It is dark all of the time. Few animals live in Antarctica. There is little food. Survival is very hard.

Stop Think Write

VOCABULARY

What detail in the first paragraph tells how chilly it is in Antarctica?

Warming Up

Spring comes in September. The days get longer. The sun shines into the sea. The sea becomes rich with small plants.

More animals come. Little animals called krill swim by. They eat the plants. Bigger fish come. They eat the plants and the krill.

Other animals come. There is plenty of food. Seals, whales, and birds hunt smaller animals. They eat krill and fish.

Sea plants

Small fish

Stop   Think   Write

COMPARE AND CONTRAST

How are the days in spring different from the days in winter?

_____

_____

_____

Summer Days

Summer begins in December. Whales **migrate** to the Antarctic waters. They feed on the krill.

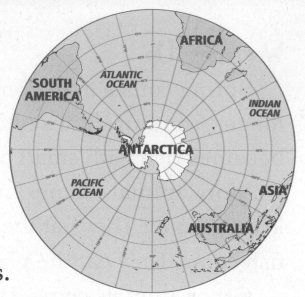

Now the sea is full of life. Flying birds come. They make nests on the shore.

Some of these birds are petrels. Petrels are like sea gulls. Their strong wings let them fly far from land. Their thick coats keep them warm. Most birds can't smell. Petrels can. They sniff out a meal.

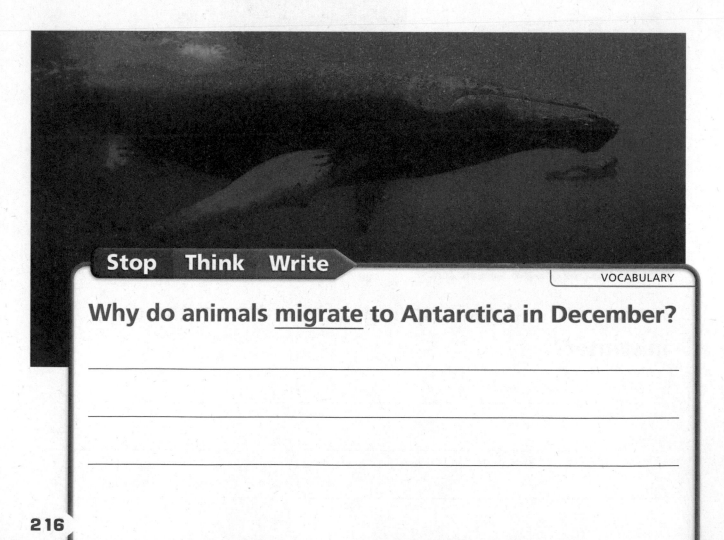

Stop   Think   Write

VOCABULARY

Why do animals migrate to Antarctica in December?

_____

_____

_____

Robin

Snow petrel

Snow Petrel Facts

Snow petrels are much smaller than other petrels. They are about the size of robins. Their feathers are white. They blend in with the snowy landscape. Only their bills, eyes, and feet are dark. When they fly, they flutter like bats.

Stop   Think   Write

MAIN IDEAS AND DETAILS

What part or parts of a snow petrel are the color of snow?

_____

_____

_____

Habits of Snow Petrels

Snow petrels are shy. If bothered, they may just fly away. If something gets too close, they have a trick. They spit out a liquid that smells very bad!

These birds fly low over the sea to find food. When they see their dinner, they dive into the water to catch it. Some birds roll in dust to clean their feathers. Snow petrels roll in the snow. That is how they clean up after they hunt.

Stop Think Write

COMPARE AND CONTRAST

Think about how some birds clean their feathers. What is different about how snow petrels do it?

_____

_____

_____

Petrel Families

A snow petrel finds a partner. Then the pair makes a nest. Like all birds, snow petrels look for a spot safe from other animals. Petrels make their nests in holes on rocky cliffs.

Most birds make their nests with leaves and grass. It's hard to find leaves or grass in Antarctica. Snow petrels line their nests with small pebbles.

The female lays one egg. Six weeks later, the chick hatches. In seven more weeks, it will fly away. It may live up to twenty years.

Stop Think Write

COMPARE AND CONTRAST

How is a snow petrel nest different from the nests of most birds?

_____

_____

_____

219

The North Pole (Arctic) and the South Pole (Antarctic)

- In this diagram, the North Pole is at the top of Earth. The South Pole is at the bottom.

- The North Pole and the South Pole stay dark during the winter. They stay light during the summer.

- The North Pole and the South Pole are very cold places.

North Pole

South Pole

When Different Seasons Begin in the North and South Poles				
	Winter	**Spring**	**Summer**	**Fall**
North Pole	December	March	June	September
South Pole	June	September	December	March

Stop Think Write

COMPARE AND CONTRAST

Write one way the North Pole and South Pole are alike. Write one way they are different.

_____

_____

_____

Look Back and Respond

1 How is life in Antarctica different in winter than in spring and summer?

Hint

For clues, see pages 214, 215, and 216.

_____

_____

_____

2 Birds, seals, and whales come to Antarctica in the summer. Why don't they live there in the winter?

Hint

For clues, see pages 214 and 220.

_____

_____

_____

3 How is the snow petrel different from other birds?

Hint

For clues, see pages 216, 217, 218, and 219.

_____

_____

_____

Return to

CYNTHIA RYLANT
The Journey
Stories of
Migration

illustrated by
LAMBERT DAVIS

"The Journey"
Student Book pp. 239–255

Be a Reading Detective!

1 **In what ways is the migration of locusts different from the migration of whales?**

☐ Locusts ride the wind; whales swim.

☐ Locusts destroy crops; whales do not.

☐ Whales migrate every year; locusts do not.

Prove It! What evidence in the selection supports your answer? Check the boxes. ☑ Make notes.

Evidence	Notes
☐ how locusts and whales travel	
☐ what locusts eat as they migrate	
☐ what causes each animal to migrate	

Write About It!

COMPARE AND CONTRAST

Answer question 1 using evidence from the text.

_____

_____

_____

_____

_____

_____

_____

2 **Why did the author write "The Journey"?**

☐ to tell readers about animal migration

☐ to tell a made-up story about whales and locusts

☐ other _____

Prove It! What evidence in the selection supports
your answer? Check the boxes. ☑ Make notes.

Evidence	Notes
☐ the introduction	
☐ facts that the author provides	
☐	

Copyright © by Houghton Mifflin Harcourt Publishing Company. All rights reserved.

Write About It!

AUTHOR'S PURPOSE

Answer question **2** **using evidence from the text.**

_____

_____

_____

_____

_____

_____

_____

✓ TARGET VOCABULARY

currently
loaded
managed
pleasure
terror

Science Fiction

Science fiction stories are about things that **currently** cannot happen. People may be **loaded** onto a spaceship. They may be flown to another planet. They may travel through time.

Writers have **managed** to make these ideas seem real. We can imagine different worlds through their stories.

We read these stories for **pleasure**. It's fun to think about different places and times. We even enjoy feeling **terror** if there are evil space creatures. That can be fun, too!

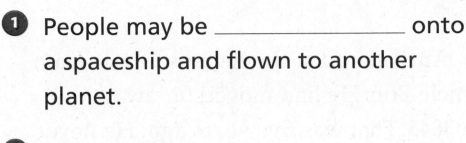

1. People may be _____ onto a spaceship and flown to another planet.

2. We may feel _____ when we read about evil space creatures.

3. We read science fiction stories for _____.

4. What are you <u>currently</u> studying in social studies?

_____

_____

_____

5. What is the most difficult thing that you have <u>managed</u> to do this year?

_____

_____

_____

Dog of the Future

by Estelle Kleinman

April stared at the big box. It was from Uncle Bob. He had moved far away in 3045. That was five years ago. He never forgot her birthday.

She opened the box. Her eyes opened wide. Uncle Bob had made a robot dog for her!

A note was in the box. April read it. She grabbed the robot dog. "I'll call you Joe," she said. She loaded Joe into her speedboat. She headed for Paco's place.

Stop   Think   Write

What does April do right before getting into her boat?

_____

_____

_____

Paco didn't think much of Joe. "A bunch of tin and screws isn't the same as a real dog," he said.

"Oink!" complained Joe.

"I guess Uncle Bob still needs to work some things out. Can you come on my boat?" asked April. "Then I can show you why Joe is so great."

"Currently, I have no other plans," Paco said. He hopped on the boat.

Stop   Think   Write

CONCLUSIONS AND GENERALIZATIONS

What part of Joe does Uncle Bob need to work on?

_____

_____

_____

"Let's take a trip," said April. "I'll show you why Joe is a good dog."

Joe took the wheel. He steered the boat away from the dock.

"Can he really control the boat?" Paco asked.

"Yes," answered April. "Uncle Bob says I just have to punch in where we want to go." Joe had a keyboard on his back. April typed in "Tower Cliffs."

Stop Think Write

SEQUENCE OF EVENTS

After Joe steers the boat away, what does April do?

_____

_____

_____

226

The water began to get very rough.

"Joe, I'm getting scared!" Paco cried with terror in his voice.

Joe slowed the boat to a crawl. A few minutes later, the boat stopped.

"That's not Tower Cliffs," Paco noted. "It's Rocky Bluff."

"Oink! Joe made a mistake," said Joe.

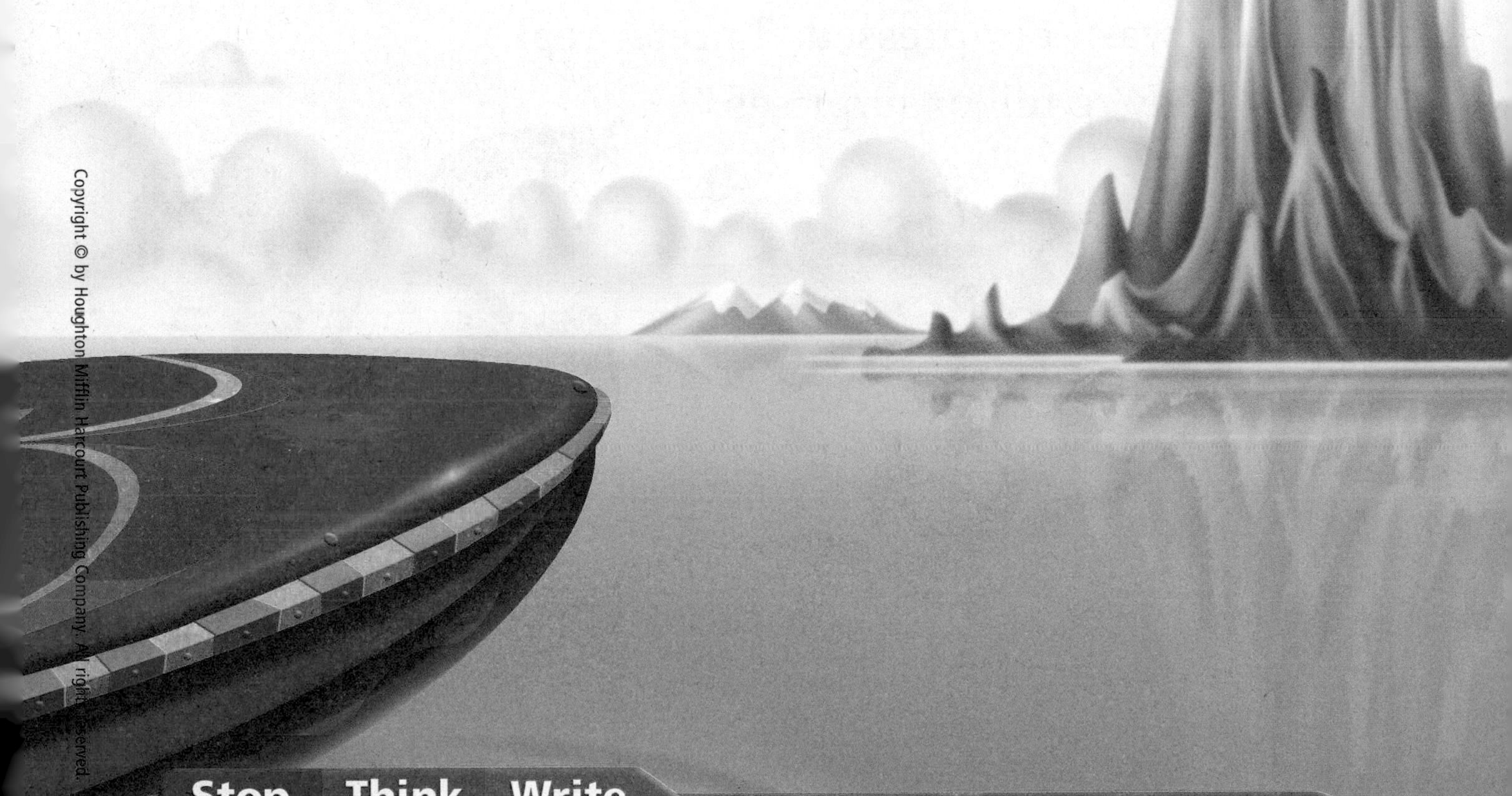

Stop Think Write

VOCABULARY

Why is there <u>terror</u> in Paco's voice?

____

____

____

"I'll tell Uncle Bob about the problems. I'm sure he can fix Joe," said April.

Joe tried again. This time he **managed** to get to Tower Cliffs. They all stepped onto the beach.

"Just watch the fancy tricks Joe can do," April said. "He can throw the ball and catch it!"

Paco wasn't impressed. "I prefer real dogs. They're full of surprises."

Stop Think Write

COMPARE AND CONTRAST

How are April and Paco different?

_____

_____

_____

Joe picked up the ball. "Should Joe throw right or left? Fast or slow?"

"How disappointing!" said Paco. "This takes the fun out of playing ball."

"Just throw the ball!" April called.

Joe threw the ball. Then he ran to make the perfect catch.

April stopped and looked around. "What's that noise?"

Paco said, "I hear yelling and barking!"

Stop Think Write

UNDERSTANDING CHARACTERS

Why is Paco disappointed with Joe?

_____

_____

_____

A brown dog ran up to April and Paco. His owner, Tina, was not far behind.

April told Tina, "We were just playing ball with my robot dog."

Tina asked if her dog Max could play. Paco threw the ball. Max ran after it. He dropped the ball at Paco's feet. Before Paco could get the ball, Joe picked it up. He threw it.

Tina laughed. "Real or robot, these two dogs are a pleasure to watch."

Stop   Think   Write

Why do you think that Tina takes pleasure in watching the dogs?

_____

_____

_____

Look Back and Respond

1 What happens at the beginning of the story?

Hint
For a clue, see page 224.

_____

_____

_____

2 After Paco hops in the boat, what does Joe do?

Hint
For clues, see pages 225 and 226.

_____

_____

_____

3 How does the story end?

Hint
For a clue, see page 230.

_____

_____

_____

Be a Reading Detective!

Return to

"The Journey of
Oliver K. Woodman"
Student Book pp. 273–295

1 **Which of the following places does Oliver visit first?**

☐ Salt Lake City ☐ Memphis

☐ Oklahoma City ☐ Dallas

Prove It! What evidence in the story supports your answer? Check the boxes. ☑ Make notes.

Evidence	Notes
☐ where each letter or postcard comes from	
☐ the date on each letter or postcard	
☐	

Write About It!

SEQUENCE OF EVENTS

Answer question 1 using evidence from the text.

_____

_____

_____

_____

_____

2 **What does everyone who writes to Uncle Ray have in common?**

☐ They all spend time with Oliver.

☐ They all think Oliver is real.

☐ They are all children.

Prove It! What evidence in the story supports your answer? Check the boxes. ☑ Make notes.

Evidence	Notes
☐ what is written in each postcard or letter	
☐ the illustrations	
☐	

Write About It!

STORY STRUCTURE

Answer question ② using evidence from the text.

_____

_____

_____

_____

_____

_____

_____

✓ **TARGET VOCABULARY**

aboard
anchor
bay
spotted
voyage

Sea Travel

1 People have always traveled across water. Today, we can fly a plane over the sea. Long ago, a sea voyage usually took place in a ship.

What do people use to make a voyage over land?

_____

_____

_____

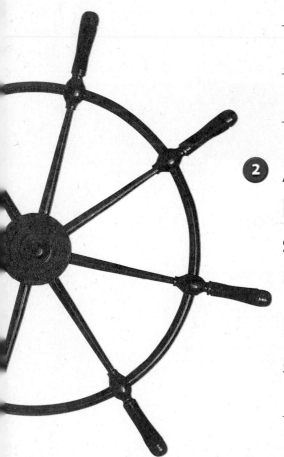

2 A ship had a crew aboard. The crew had to know many things. They studied how the winds moved. They used the sails to catch the wind.

How do you think you would feel aboard a ship?

_____

_____

_____

3 Ships sailed on open waters. Weeks might pass before the crew spotted land.

What is another way to say spotted?

_____

4 They usually looked for a bay. Land around the bay kept the ship safe from winds and waves.

Why is a bay a safe place for a ship?

_____

_____

_____

5 The crew would drop an anchor into the water. It held the ship in place. The crew rowed to land in a small boat.

Why must an anchor be heavy?

_____

_____

_____

To the South Seas

by Margaret Maugenest

In the late 1700s, there were few maps of the South Seas. Scientists in England wanted to know about the land in the South Pacific. Was there a huge continent there? Some people thought there was. They asked Captain James Cook to go find out.

Stop Think Write

What clues on this page tell you that this story contains facts?

_____

_____

_____

An ocean trip was long. It was hard. There were many dangers. The seas could get stormy. Pirates could attack. A fire could break out. There was no way to get help.

Cook and his crew got ready for the **voyage**. They filled the ship with supplies. They took fresh water. They took food. They had a goat for milk.

England

Tahiti

Cook's Voyage

Stop Think Write

AUTHOR'S PURPOSE

Look at the picture. What does it show you?

_____

_____

_____

Setting Sail

Ninety-five crew members were 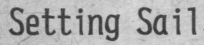. Each person on the ship had a certain job.

The ship left England in 1789. It sailed west. It crossed the Atlantic. It went around the tip of South America. A huge storm came up! Five of the men died.

Stop Think Write

STORY STRUCTURE

What happened as the ship went around the tip of South America?

_____

_____

_____

The ship sailed for ten more weeks. The men started to run out of food. They did not want to starve. They caught fish to stay alive.

They went through the South Pacific. The men finally spotted Tahiti. The men were happy. They could not wait to reach the island. They had been at sea for eight months.

Stop Think Write

VOCABULARY

How long had the men been at sea when they spotted Tahiti?

_____

_____

_____

Land, Ho!

The ship sailed into a bay. The crew dropped the anchor. This held the ship in place. Then the crew got into a smaller boat. They rowed to land.

At first, the people who lived there were uneasy. They did not know Captain Cook. They wanted to know what Cook wanted. Soon they became friendly.

Stop Think Write

VOCABULARY

Why was the <u>anchor</u> dropped when the ship was near land?

_____

_____

_____

Cook stayed in Tahiti for three months. He made a map of the island. His scientists studied the plants there.

Then Cook sailed on. He explored the South Seas more. He looked for a huge continent. He did not find one. Cook did see a smaller continent. It was Australia. Mapmakers now had to make new maps.

Stop | Think | Write

SEQUENCE OF EVENTS

What did Cook do after he left Tahiti?

Cook's Maps

Cook made two more sea trips. He changed old maps. He showed places where he had been. He made many new maps. He made a map of the west coast of North America. It went all the way up to Alaska.

Other explorers used his maps. There used to be many different maps of the same land. Cook's maps made travel less confusing. They also made travel safer.

Stop **Think** **Write**

CONCLUSIONS

How did Captain Cook help future explorers?

_____

_____

_____

Look Back and Respond

1 **Why did Cook set sail in 1789?**

Hint

For clues, see pages 234 and 236.

_____

_____

_____

2 **How did the people of Tahiti act towards Captain Cook and his crew ?**

Hint

For clues, see page 238.

_____

_____

_____

3 **What did Captain Cook find out about the continent in the South Seas?**

Hint

For a clue, see page 239.

_____

_____

_____

Be a Reading Detective!

1 Why did the author write "Dog-of-the-Sea-Waves"?

☐ to show that seals make good pets

☐ to tell a story of how people came to Hawaii

☐ other _____

Prove It! What evidence in the story supports your answer? Check the boxes. 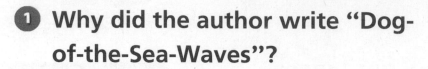   Make notes.

Evidence	Notes
☐ why the brothers come to the island	
☐ how the story ends	
☐	

Write About It!

AUTHOR'S PURPOSE

Answer question **1** using evidence from the text.

_____

_____

_____

_____

_____

_____

_____

2 Which word best describes Manu?

- ☐ grouchy
- ☐ serious
- ☐ helpful
- ☐ kind

Prove It! What evidence in the story supports your answer? Check the boxes. ☑ Make notes.

Evidence	Notes
☐ what Manu does for his brothers	
☐ what Manu does for Dog-of-the-Sea-Waves	

Write About It!

UNDERSTANDING CHARACTERS

Answer question 2 using evidence from the text.

_____

_____

_____

_____

_____

_____

_____

Outdoor Gear

✓ TARGET VOCABULARY

**altitude
avalanches
equipment
increases
slopes**

❶ Mountain climbing is a fun sport. Still, it is important to stay safe. Special gear can help climbers in avalanches. A long red cord can mark where a climber is trapped under snow.

What other equipment might help a climber in <u>avalanches</u>?

_____

_____

_____

❷ The sun can be strong at a high altitude. You should wear sunscreen to protect your skin.

Have you ever been at a high <u>altitude</u>? What was it like?

_____

_____

_____

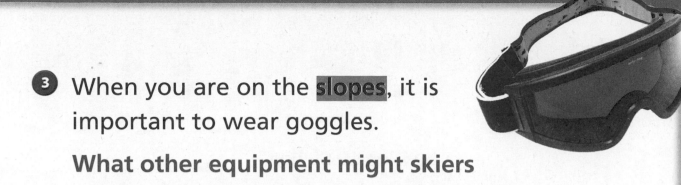

3 When you are on the slopes, it is important to wear goggles.

What other equipment might skiers need when they are on the <u>slopes</u>?

_____

_____

_____

4 Danger increases when you do not have the right safety gear.

What <u>increases</u> your chance of getting a good seat at the movies?

_____

_____

_____

5 One piece of equipment that helps a climber find his way is a compass.

Name another piece of <u>equipment</u> a climber could use.

_____

Ski Patrol

by Dina McClellan

The men and women of the ski patrol do important work. They risk their lives to keep people safe.

Blizzards

One job of the ski patrol is to help people in blizzards. Blizzards are bad news for skiers. Strong winds can make skiers fall. Ice and snow make it hard for them to see.

Stop **Think** **Write**

TEXT AND GRAPHIC FEATURES

What is the title of this text?

_____

_____

_____

Avalanches

Avalanches happen when a huge chunk of snow slides down a mountain. People can get trapped inside the snow. They need help to get out.

The ski patrol has dogs. They are trained to find people in the snow. First the dogs find where the people are trapped. Then the ski patrol works fast to dig them out.

Stop | **Think** | **Write**

VOCABULARY

How do you think dogs find people in avalanches?

_____

_____

_____

What happens after a person is dug out? The person may be hurt. The ski patrol is trained to do first aid. They give care on the spot.

Some hurt people need even more help. The ski patrol moves these people off the slopes. They use helicopters, sleds, and snowmobiles. They get people to a hospital fast!

Stop　Think　Write

Why can't ambulances go on the slopes?

_____

_____

_____

Snow Gear

The men and women of the ski patrol have special **equipment**. They always wear bright clothing. That way people can recognize them.

Skiers should wear bright clothing, too. If they are lost, bright clothing **increases** their chances of being seen. Then they can get help.

Stop Think Write

CONCLUSIONS AND GENERALIZATIONS

What colors are most easily seen in snow?

_____

_____

_____

Ski Patrol Schedule

Mornings are busy for the ski patrol. They check mountain trails. They mark spots that aren't safe. They warn people about dangers that may occur at such a high altitude.

During the day, the ski patrol checks trails again. They look to see if anyone is lost, hurt, or trapped.

Stop Think Write

MAIN IDEAS AND DETAILS

Why does the ski patrol check mountain trails?

_____

_____

_____

The ski patrol works long hours. They must be sure that every skier is off the mountain at the end of the day. They make sure everyone is safe. Only then can they rest!

Stop **Think** **Write**

INFER AND PREDICT

How do you think the men and women of the ski patrol feel at the end the day?

_____

_____

_____

Things a Skier Might Need

Large orange plastic bag

This can attract attention. You can also climb into it to stay dry.

Ski helmet

This can protect your head while you ski.

Whistle

This can attract attention. Three blasts is a signal for help.

Compass

This helps you find your way if you are lost.

Goggles

These are important for seeing in the bright snow.

Fleece vest

This helps you stay warm.

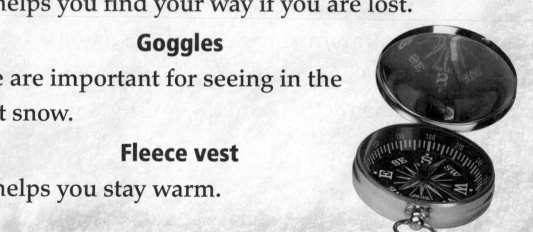

Stop · Think · Write

TEXT AND GRAPHIC FEATURES

Which two items on the list have the same purpose?

_____

_____

_____

Look Back and Respond

1 **What do the headings in this text tell you about?**

_____

_____

_____

Hint

To answer this question, look on pages 244, 245, 247, and 248.

2 **What is page 245 mostly about?**

_____

_____

_____

Hint

Look at the heading.

3 **How does the ski patrol help people who are hurt?**

_____

_____

_____

Hint

For a clue, see page 246.

Be a Reading Detective!

Return to

"Mountains"
Student Book pp. 347–363

1 What does the selection tell you about mountain climbing equipment?

☐ information about protective equipment

☐ information about oxygen

☐ information about tools

Prove It! What evidence in the selection supports your answer? Check the boxes. ☑ Make notes.

Evidence	Notes
☐ the text	
☐ photos and captions	
☐ boxed features with more facts	

Write About It!

TEXT AND GRAPHIC FEATURES

Answer question **1** using evidence from the text.

_____

_____

_____

_____

_____

_____

2 **In what ways was Temba's second climb different from his first?**

☐ He was more experienced.

☐ He had the right equipment.

☐ He climbed with a team.

Prove It! What evidence in the selection supports your answer? Check the boxes. ☑ Make notes.

Evidence	Notes
☐ details about his first climb	
☐ details about his second climb	
☐	

Write About It!

COMPARE AND CONTRAST

Answer question 2 using evidence from the text.

_____

_____

_____

_____

_____

_____

The Early Days of Cars

1 Owning a car was rare in 1900. Most people used horses to travel. Few people could buy a car. They were proud of the new machines.

What is something you are proud of?

_____

_____

_____

2 The first cars did not have the ability to go fast. They often broke down. Tires went flat, and roads were bumpy.

What is an ability that you need to do well in school? Explain.

_____

_____

_____

3 Before a long car trip, a driver would listen to people's **advice**. He made sure to bring extra tires and lots of supplies.

How is giving <u>advice</u> different from giving an order?

_____

_____

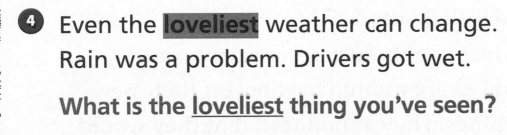

4 Even the **loveliest** weather can change. Rain was a problem. Drivers got wet.

What is the <u>loveliest</u> thing you've seen?

_____

_____

_____

5 Drivers often brought a friend along. The friend **announced** any dangers.

What is something your principal <u>announced</u>?

_____

The Race of 1903

by Dina McClellan

The first cars were made over 100 years ago. They weren't called cars. They were called autos.

Most people had never seen an auto. Automakers wanted to show off their new machines. They announced that they would hold a race.

Stop Think Write

VOCABULARY

How do you think people felt when automakers <u>announced</u> they would hold a race?

_____

_____

_____

A Race Across the Country

The Great Race took place in 1903. The race was across the whole country. It started in San Francisco. It ended in New York.

The cars in the race only had front seats. They had no windshields. The cars did not have the **ability** to go fast. They only went about thirty miles per hour. Still, most people thought the cars were amazing.

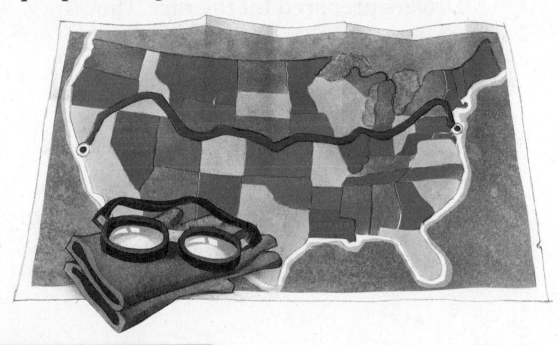

Stop **Think** **Write**

VOCABULARY

What is an <u>ability</u> cars have now that the first cars did not?

_____

_____

_____

Drivers prepared for the race. They packed food, water, and tools. They had tarps for the rain. They planned the best route.

They did not want to make sharp turns. They did not want to cross ditches. Those things slowed drivers down. They wanted to go fast. There was a prize for the winner.

Stop Think Write

MAIN IDEA AND DETAILS

What did drivers do to prepare for the long trip?

_____

_____

_____

They're Off!

The race began on one of the **loveliest** mornings in June. Crowds lined the streets of San Francisco. Bands played. The mayor gave a speech. The cars lined up. They were ready to go.

Then the cars took off! Some went off the roads. This was dangerous. A car could run into a ditch. It might break down.

Stop   Think   Write

MAIN IDEA AND DETAILS

What took place before the start of the race?

_____

_____

_____

Rough Roads

Sometimes roads were bad. Then the drivers had to slow down. They sped up when the roads were good. The cars made the air dusty. The cars did not have windshields. Each person in the car had to wear goggles.

Cars often got flat tires. Their engines broke. Then the cars needed to be fixed. Drivers fell behind in the race.

Stop **Think** **Write**

MAIN IDEA AND DETAILS

What made the trip difficult? Name some things that could go wrong.

_____

_____

_____

Along the Way

People came to watch and shout **advice**.
They cheered as the cars drove by.

Some drivers tried to collect money. They
did this by giving people rides in their cars.
Then they bought more supplies for the trip.

Stop **Think** **Write**

MAKE INFERENCES

Why would people pay money just to ride in a car?

_____

_____

_____

Reaching the Finish

The race lasted for two months. At last the drivers reached New York. They were covered in mud. They were tired. Still, they were proud.

The Great Race of 1903 was big news. It made people think that the auto was more than a neat machine. It was a great way to travel.

Stop Think Write

MAKE PREDICTIONS

What do you think happened as a result of the car's new popularity?

Look Back and Respond

1 How were cars of the past different from the cars of today?

_____

_____

_____

Hint

For clues, see pages 255 and 258.

2 What could make drivers lose time in the race?

_____

_____

_____

Hint

For clues, see pages 256, 257, and 258.

3 Why was the race important?

_____

_____

_____

Hint

For clues, see pages 254 and 260.

Be a Reading Detective!

1 **What is the main idea on page 12 of "The Foot Race Across America"?**

☐ Fifty-five runners completed the race.

☐ The runners had to run twenty extra miles.

☐ One day, the runners ran seventy-five miles.

Prove It! What evidence in the selection supports your answer? Check the boxes. ☑ Make notes.

Evidence	Notes
☐ a sentence that states the main idea	
☐ details that support the main idea	
☐	

Write About It!

MAIN IDEA AND DETAILS

Answer question 1 using evidence from the text.

_____

_____

_____

_____

_____

_____

_____

2 **Why did Andy Payne run in the foot race?**

☐ His friend John Salo encouraged him to enter.

☐ He wanted to win money to help his parents.

☐ other _____

Prove It! What evidence in the selection supports
your answer? Check the boxes. ☑ Make notes.

Evidence	Notes
☐ events in the 1920s	
☐ details about the race	
☐ details about Andy Payne	

NEW MEXICO
US
66

Write About It!

CAUSE AND EFFECT

Answer question 2 using evidence from the text.

_____

_____

_____

_____

_____

_____

261B

experiment
familiar
improve
invention
research

Machines with Magnets

Magnets are found in many machines. Some machines are familiar. They are things you know. A doorbell has magnets. An invention such as a computer has magnets. A hair dryer has magnets.

Sometimes scientists want to make a new machine. They learn the science of how magnets work. They do research. They think of how to use magnets to make something new.

Will the new machine work? Scientists do an experiment. They test the machine. Then they try to improve it. It must work well. When it does, people can use it.

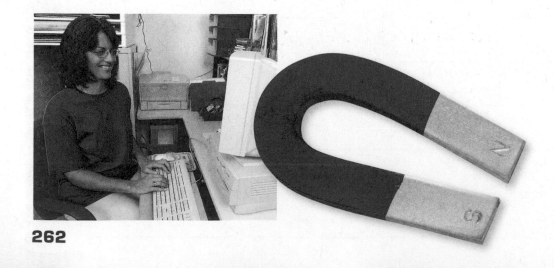

1 A new _____ might be

a machine that uses magnets.

2 First, scientists test the new

machine. Then they find ways to

_____ it.

3 Machines you see every day are

_____ to you.

4 Scientists do _____ to

learn about something. They learn facts

that help them make something new.

5 Scientists try out inventions. They

might do an _____ to

see if a new invention works.

The Boy Who Made the TV
by Cate Foley

Have you heard of Philo T. Farnsworth? If not, don't worry. Many people are not familiar with him. Philo Farnsworth made a popular invention. He made the modern television. He was just fourteen years old when he got the idea.

Stop   Think   Write

What <u>invention</u> did Philo Farnsworth make?

_____

_____

_____

Farm Boy

Philo was born in Utah in 1906. He helped work on his family's farm.

Philo's parents wanted to **improve** their lives. They moved the family to a new farm in Idaho. In the attic, Philo found science magazines. They would change his life.

Stop   Think   Write

MAKE PREDICTIONS

Predict how the magazines changed Philo's life.

_____

_____

_____

Philo's Idea

Philo read the magazines. He learned about something called electrons. He read about a new idea. People wanted to use electrons to send pictures through the air.

One day Philo was plowing a field. He thought about electrons. He wondered if they could go back and forth like the plow. Maybe electrons could read pictures line by line! This was a new idea.

Stop   Think   Write

CAUSE AND EFFECT

How did plowing a field help Philo get a new idea about electrons?

_____

_____

_____

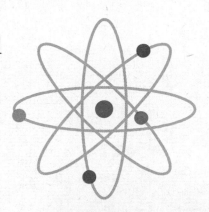

Television was different then. One kind showed a picture on a wall. Philo had a new idea. He wanted to make an electron tube. It would make pictures by shooting electrons at a special screen.

Philo worked hard on his idea. He tried one experiment after another. Some of his teachers helped. They tried new ways of making the tube. The more they tried, the more they learned.

Stop   Think   Write

VOCABULARY

Why do you think Philo had to conduct more than one experiment?

_____

_____

_____

Success!

Finally, the tube was ready. Philo tried to send an image. Can you guess what image he sent? It was a dollar sign.

The tube worked! Philo sent a television image. It was like the ones we see today. He was just twenty-one years old. His research and testing were successful. He had made a new kind of television.

Stop   Think   Write

VOCABULARY

How did Philo's <u>research</u> and testing lead to success?

_____

_____

_____

TV Catches On

Television was getting popular. A large company said that it had invented the new electron tube. A court said that Philo was the inventor.

Philo did not always like television. He thought many shows were bad. Still, television showed important events, too. In 1969, Philo saw the first man walk on the Moon. Before, he would have read this news.

Stop   Think   Write

CAUSE AND EFFECT

How did television change the way people learned news?

_____

_____

_____

A Great Inventor

Philo made other inventions. He helped create radar. He thought of a machine that hospitals used to help babies. He found new ways for people to get electricity. He created over 300 inventions!

Philo Farnsworth died in 1971. Today, almost every home has a television. A magazine said Philo was one of the most important people of the twentieth century. Would you agree?

Stop Think Write

CAUSE AND EFFECT

Why did a magazine say that Philo was one of the most important people of the twentieth century?

_____

_____

_____

Look Back and Respond

1 How did Philo become interested in science?

_____

_____

_____

Hint
For a clue, see pages 265 and 266.

2 Why was Philo critical of television?

_____

_____

_____

Hint
For clues, see page 269.

3 Do you think Philo cared about helping people? Explain.

_____

_____

_____

Hint
For clues, see page 270.

Be a Reading Detective!

Return to

The
POWER
of Magnets

"The Power of Magnets"
Student Magazine pp. 20–25

1 Why can you turn an electromagnet off?

☐ The poles repel each other.

☐ It only works when it has electricity.

☐ Moving a coil produces electricity.

Prove It! What evidence in the selection supports your answer? Check the boxes. ☑ Make notes.

Evidence	Notes
☐ how junkyards use electromagnets	
☐ photos and captions	
☐	

Write About It!

CAUSE AND EFFECT

Answer question **1** using evidence from the text.

_____

_____

_____

_____

_____

_____

_____

_____

2 **Why did the author write "The Power of Magnets"?**

☐ to show that motors are used in many appliances

☐ to tell the life story of Michael Faraday

☐ to explain about magnets and electricity

Prove It! What evidence in the selection supports your answer? Check the boxes. ☑ Make notes.

Evidence	Notes
☐ details about how magnets work	
☐ details about how magnets are used	
☐ diagrams and photos	

Write About It!

AUTHOR'S PURPOSE

Answer question ② using evidence from the text.

_____

_____

_____

_____

_____

_____

✓ **TARGET VOCABULARY**

**landscape
peak
slopes
steep
textures**

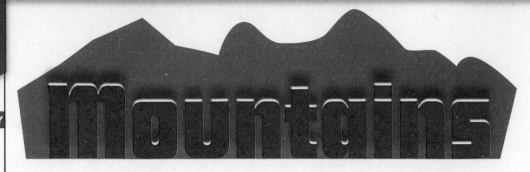

1 The landscape is beautiful. You can see mountains. You can see forests. You can see a river.

Describe the kind of landscape you like best.

_____

_____

_____

2 The mountains are steep. It is hard to climb to the top.

Name something other than a mountain that can be steep.

_____

_____

3 In winter, there is snow. People ski on the slopes.

Which slopes are best for fast skiing—steep ones or gentle ones?

_____

4 Look at that tall peak! Snow covers the top of the mountain.

Write a synonym for peak.

_____

5 Snow and ice have different textures. Some snow is light and fluffy. Ice is hard and smooth.

Compare the textures of sandpaper and silk.

_____

_____

Climbing the Slopes

by Mia Lewis

It is a sunny day in the Green Mountains. A group of students arrive at a lodge. The landscape is beautiful.

"Hi!" says a young man. "I'm Javier. This is Karen. We are going to teach you about rock climbing. We'll also teach you how to find your way in the forest. You'll have a lot of fun this week!"

Stop Think Write

FACT AND OPINION

Javier says, "You'll have a lot of fun this week!" Is that a fact or an opinion? Explain.

_____

_____

_____

The group meets inside a building. It has a climbing wall. The wall looks like a rock. The wall has different **textures**.

"There's a lot to learn," says Karen. "We're going to practice first."

"That wall is too **steep**," says Teo.

"You'll do fine," says Javier. "You just have to practice."

Stop   Think   Write

VOCABULARY

How do you think Teo feels when he looks at the steep wall?

_____

_____

_____

275

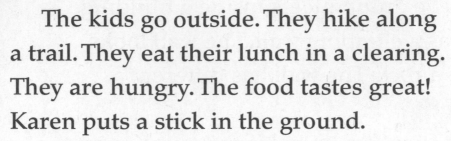

The kids go outside. They hike along a trail. They eat their lunch in a clearing. They are hungry. The food tastes great! Karen puts a stick in the ground.

"What are you doing?" asks Maya.

"I'm going to find out where north, east, south, and west are," she says.

"My cell phone is better. It can show where we are. It has maps," says Teo.

Stop Think Write

What part of what Teo says is fact? What part is his opinion?

_____

_____

_____

"A cell phone could lose power," says Latoya. "Then it can't help at all."

"We can use the sun to tell directions," says Karen. "See the shadow of the stick? Let's mark the tip of the shadow with a pebble. Now we wait awhile."

Stop Think Write

STORY STRUCTURE

What is the problem with depending on Teo's cell phone to tell directions?

_____

_____

_____

277

They check after ten minutes. The shadow has moved. Karen puts a pebble where the tip of the shadow is now. She draws a line between the two pebbles.

"The shadow moved because the sun moved," she says. "The sun moves west. Shadows move east. We know which way the shadow moved. So we know which way is east. Now we can follow any directions we have!"

Stop   Think   Write

CAUSE AND EFFECT

Why does the stick's shadow move?

_____

_____

_____

The next day the students meet again. They stand at the bottom of some rocky slopes. Javier is with them. Teo looks worried.

"Are these ropes safe?" he says.

"They are very safe," says Javier. "You did well on the climbing wall. Give it a try. I'll be here to help."

Stop   Think   Write

VOCABULARY

Why is Teo worried when he looks at the mountain slopes?

_____

_____

_____

279

A few days later, it is time to go home! Time has passed too quickly.

"I learned so much!" says Maya. "I am going to miss this camp."

"We will miss you, too," says Karen.

"I wish I had time for one last climb," says Teo. "I feel as if I could reach the peak of the mountain!"

"You'll just have to come back soon," says Javier.

Stop Think Write

FACT AND OPINION

Read this sentence: "Time has passed too quickly." Is that a fact or an opinion? Explain your answer.

_____

_____

_____

Look Back and Respond

1 Teo says the climbing wall is too steep. Is that a fact or his opinion?

_____

_____

_____

2 Name a person in the story who mostly expresses opinions. Write one opinion that he or she says.

_____

_____

_____

3 Name a person in the story who mostly states facts. Write one fact that he or she says.

_____

_____

_____

Be a Reading Detective!

1 Which opinion can you support with facts from the text?

"Becoming Anything He Wants to Be" Student Magazine pp. 34–39

☐ It is too hard for blind people to do sports.

☐ A blind person can do anything.

☐ It is amazing what blind people can achieve.

Prove It! What evidence in the selection supports your answer? Check the boxes. ☑ Make notes.

Evidence	Notes
☐ details about Erik as a child	
☐ details about Erik as an adult	
☐ photos and captions	

Write About It!

FACT AND OPINION

Answer question **1** using evidence from the text.

_____

_____

_____

_____

_____

_____

2 **Which of these events took place the most recently?**

☐ Erik climbs Mount Everest.

☐ Erik teaches around the world.

☐ Erik becomes captain of a wrestling team.

Prove It! What evidence in the selection supports your answer? Check the boxes. ☑ Make notes.

Evidence	Notes
☐ what Erik did in school	
☐ what Erik does now	
☐ Erik's adventures	

Write About It!

SEQUENCE OF EVENTS

Answer question ② using evidence from the text.

_____

_____

_____

_____

_____

_____

_____

Working Hard and Having Fun

An **athlete** is someone who plays a sport. Soccer players are athletes. So are tennis players. Athletes train hard to **succeed**. They go to practice. They go to games. They push themselves.

Some athletes try out for a sports team. They must **earn** a spot on the team. Then the players work together to win.

Often, fans **contribute** to the way a team plays. They cheer loudly for their team. This makes players work harder. It also adds **excitement** to the event.

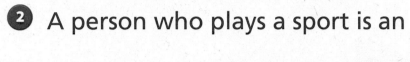

1 Each player works hard to

_____ to a win for

the team.

2 A person who plays a sport is an

_____ .

3 Athletes practice to

_____ at doing

their best.

4 How does the <u>excitement</u> of a
cheering crowd affect the players
on a team?

_____

_____

_____

5 Why must players <u>earn</u> a spot on some
sports teams?

_____

_____

Sprinting Joyce

by Mia Lewis

Joyce had a big brother. His name was Roy. He drove her to school each day. When they arrived, he always said the same thing.

"See you later, slowpoke!"

This was starting to bug Joyce. She had joined the track team. Her coach didn't think she was a slowpoke!

Stop Think Write

UNDERSTANDING CHARACTERS

How does Roy act toward Joyce?

_____

_____

_____

Joyce told her friend Leslie what was going on.

"Roy is the sports editor of the school paper," said Leslie. "I'll write some articles about the team. I'll give you a nickname. I'll say you are a great **athlete**. Roy won't know it's you. Once he finds out, he'll know you aren't a slowpoke."

Joyce smiled. "This sounds like fun!"

Stop Think Write

CAUSE AND EFFECT

How could Leslie's plan change Roy's mind?

_____

_____

_____

Leslie told her plan to the track team.
"From now on," she said, "Joyce will be SJ.
It stands for Sprinting Joyce. Don't tell Roy!"
"Your secret is safe!" said Meg and Rita.
"You just have to run fast, Joyce!" said
Leslie. "Then our plan will succeed."
"I'll try!" said Joyce.

Stop   Think   Write

MAKE INFERENCES

Why does Leslie tell the other teammates about the plan?

_____

_____

_____

SJ Makes Team

by Leslie Chin

What's the buzz around school? It's about our girls' track team. They are fast, and they keep winning. They may even **earn** a spot at the state track meet!

The rising star is SJ. This sprinter is no slowpoke! She can **contribute** more speed to the team. SJ will help them win.

Stop Think Write

VOCABULARY

Why do you think the team must <u>earn</u> a spot at the state track meet?

_____

_____

_____

"Now I have to win!" said Joyce.

"Don't worry," said Leslie. "Just don't tell Roy how fast you run. He'll be so surprised!"

Just then, Roy walked by their table.

"Who is this SJ?" he asked.

"You must be kidding!" Meg said. "Everybody knows SJ!"

Stop   Think   Write

CONCLUSIONS

How can you tell that Joyce is a fast runner?

_____

_____

_____

SPORTS

Track Coach Predicts Victory

by Leslie Chin

Get set for a big win! Our girls' track team is filled with <mark>excitement</mark>. SJ is heating up the track. We're all rooting for her!

The coach is happy, too. "I think SJ will take us to the top," she said.

"I wish I could tell Roy," said Joyce. "He thinks I'm warming the bench."

"Just run," said Leslie.

Stop   Think   Write

VOCABULARY

What does Leslie mean when she writes that the girls' track team is filled with <u>excitement</u>?

_____

_____

_____

289

It was time for their next race. Joyce led the team to a big win.

"Did you know that SJ is short for Sprinting Joyce?" Leslie asked Roy.

Roy smiled. "I won't call you slowpoke anymore," he said. "I promise!"

Joyce was happy. Leslie wrote about the race. She chose a headline for the story: "Winning Team Gets Cheers from Roy!"

Stop Think Write

Why does Joyce feel happy now?

_____

_____

_____

Look Back and Respond

1 **How does Roy bother Joyce?**

Hint

For a clue, see page 284.

_____

_____

_____

2 **Write two words to describe Leslie.**

Hint

Think about Leslie's plan and her stories.

_____

_____

_____

3 **Write three words to describe Roy.**

Hint

Think about how Roy acts at the beginning and at the end.

_____

_____

_____

4 **Write a title of your own for Leslie's final story.**

Hint

Think about what happens in the story.

_____

_____

_____

Be a Reading Detective!

1 **What can you tell about Manny?**

☐ He wants to be liked.

☐ He is a team player.

☐ He likes to brag.

"A New Team of Heroes"
Student Magazine pp. 48–55

Prove It! What evidence in the play supports your answer? Check the boxes. ☑   Make notes.

Evidence	Notes
☐ what Manny says	
☐ what the narrator says about Manny	
☐ what other players say about Manny	

Write About It!

UNDERSTANDING CHARACTERS

Answer question **1** using evidence from the text.

_____

_____

_____

_____

_____

_____

2 How does Manny help the Hawks win?

☐ He figures out how to score on the other team.

☐ He kicks in two goals to win the game.

☐ He replaces Carla, who is too tired to score.

Prove It! What evidence in the play supports your answer? Check the boxes. ☑ Make notes.

Evidence	Notes
☐ what Manny says and does	
☐ what Carla says and does	
☐ how the second goal is scored	

Write About It!

STORY STRUCTURE

Answer question **2** using evidence from the text.

_____

_____

_____

_____

_____

_____

✓ TARGET VOCABULARY

afford
applause
certainly
raise
worried

Raising Money for a Friend

It was my friend Rosa's birthday. Rosa loves to draw. Eddie and I wanted to give her crayons. We could not afford to buy them. We were worried. What could we do?

We decided to raise money. We sold lemonade. It was so tasty! We certainly had lots of customers. We earned money, too.

Eddie and I got the crayons. Rosa clapped when she saw them. We didn't buy crayons to get applause. We just wanted to make Rosa happy.

1 Eddie and I could not _____

to buy crayons.

2 We were _____ about

not having money.

3 We did not buy a gift to get

_____ .

4 What is one thing you will <u>certainly</u> do
next summer?

_____

_____

_____

5 What are some things you can do to
<u>raise</u> money?

_____

_____

_____

The Rockets

by Candyce Norvell

It was the beginning of the season. Coach Gema was giving the Rockets a speech.

"There are three things we need for a winning team," he said. "We need practice. We need discipline. We need teamwork. I want you all to work with the team. Don't try to be a star on your own. Remember, there's no *I* in *team*."

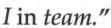 **Stop   Think   Write**

CONCLUSIONS

Why does Coach Gema want the Rockets to remember that there is no *I* in *team*?

_____

_____

_____

294

The team worked hard at practice. Soon they were working well as a team. They even won their first game!

Coach Gema was proud. Then he heard some team members brag. "I don't like bragging. Remember what I told you," he said. "There is no *I* in *team.*"

Stop Think Write

CONCLUSIONS

Why doesn't Coach Gema want the team members to show off?

_____

_____

_____

One day, Emily told her friend Lupe bad news. Emily had to quit the team. "My mom is sick," Emily said. "My family needs me at home. We all need to help out. We can't afford to pay someone else."

"The team will be sorry to lose you," said Lupe. "You are a great player."

Lupe told the team about Emily.

"I am worried about Emily and her family," said Will. "Can the team help?"

Stop | Think | Write

VOCABULARY

Why is Will worried?

_____

_____

_____

"I know a group that helps families," Anders said. "Maybe we can raise money for that group."

"That's a great idea," said Coach Gema. "What should we do?"

"How about a car wash?" said Sovann. "We could have it this weekend."

The whole team agreed.

Charity Car Wash
This Saturday
Wash & Dry
$3.00

Stop **Think** **Write**

CONCLUSIONS

How do the Rockets feel about Sovann's idea to have a car wash?

_____

_____

_____

On Saturday, the team brought supplies. They washed cars all day. They raised a lot of money. They gave the money to the group that would help Emily's family.

Coach Gema was proud of the Rockets. "You remembered that there is no *I* in *team*," he said.

"Maybe we can earn more money. Let's have a car wash next weekend, too," said Anders.

Stop   Think   Write

INFER AND PREDICT

What do you think the Rockets will do next?

_____

_____

_____

When the season ended, the Rockets went to the school sports dinner.

"There are two more awards to give out," said the principal. "One award is for a team that raised money to help someone. The other award is for the best teamwork. Both awards go to the Rockets! They remembered that there's no *I* in *team*."

Everyone clapped. The Rockets listened to the applause. They were proud.

Stop Think Write

VOCABULARY

Why does the applause make the Rockets feel proud?

_____

_____

_____

Later that week, the Rockets went out for pizza.

"I want olives!" said Anders.

"I want extra cheese!" said Lupe.

"I want hot peppers!" Sovann said.

"Not peppers! I want sausage," said Will.

"Hey!" said Coach Gema. "What about teamwork?"

"Coach," Will said, "there is no *I* in *team*, but there is certainly an *I* in *pizza*!"

Stop | **Think** | **Write**

How do the Rockets act at the pizza place?

_____

_____

_____

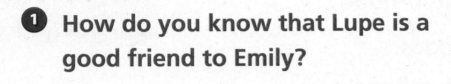 **Look Back and Respond**

1 How do you know that Lupe is a good friend to Emily?

Hint
For clues, see page 296.

_____

_____

_____

2 What shows you that the Rockets know how to work as a team?

Hint
For clues, see pages 295 and 298.

_____

_____

_____

3 Would you like to play for the Rockets? Why or why not?

Hint
Think about how the team members treat each other.

_____

_____

_____

Be a Reading Detective!

Return to

SAVING BUSTER

"Saving Buster"
Student Magazine pp. 66–73

1 What do you learn about the people in Donovan's neighborhood?

- ☐ They all have dogs.
- ☐ They help each other out.
- ☐ They compete at everything.

Prove It! What evidence in the story supports your answer? Check the boxes. ☑ Make notes.

Evidence	Notes
☐ what happens before the contest	
☐ what happens at the contest	
☐	

Write About It!

CONCLUSIONS

Answer question **1** using evidence from the text.

_____

_____

_____

_____

_____

_____

_____

2 How do the neighbors raise enough money for the vet bill?

☐ from the contest

☐ from the banker and other businesses

☐ from both of the above

Prove It! What evidence in the story supports your answer? Check the boxes. ☑ Make notes.

Evidence	Notes
☐ Donovan's idea	
☐ what Carl Baca says	
☐ how the story ends	

Write About It!

CAUSE AND EFFECT

Answer question **2** using evidence from the text.

_____

_____

_____

_____

_____

_____

_____

Summarize Strategy

You can **summarize** what you read.

• Tell important ideas in your own words.

• Tell ideas in an order that makes sense.

• Keep the meaning of the text.

• Use only a few sentences.

Analyze/Evaluate Strategy

You can **analyze** and **evaluate** a text. Think carefully about what you read. Form an opinion about it.

1. Think about the text and the author.

   - What are the important facts and ideas?

   - What does the author want you to know?

2. Decide what is important. Then form an opinion.

   - How do you feel about what you read?

   - Do you agree with the author's ideas?

Infer/Predict Strategy

Use clues to figure out what the author does not tell you. Then you are making an **inference**.

Use clues to figure out what will happen next. Then you are making a **prediction**.

Monitor/Clarify Strategy

Monitor what you read. Make sure it makes sense.

Find a way to understand what does not make sense.

• Reread.

• Read ahead.

• Ask questions.

Question Strategy

Ask yourself **questions** as you read.

Look for answers.

Some questions to ask:
- What does the author mean?
- Who or what is this about?
- Why did this happen?
- What is the main idea?

Visualize Strategy

You can **visualize**.
- Make pictures in your mind as you read.
- Use words in the text to help you.
- Make pictures of people, places, things, and actions.

PHOTO CREDITS